The New Women Consumers of Asia

To dear Joyce & Don:

Cheers,

[signature]

HOLDING UP HALF OF THE SKY
The New Women Consumers of Asia

Yuwa Hedrick-Wong

John Wiley & Sons (Asia) Pte., Ltd

Copyright © 2006 by Yuwa Hedrick-Wong
Published in 2006 by John Wiley & Sons (Asia) Pte Ltd
2 Clementi Loop, #02-01, Singapore 129809

All rights reserved.

No part of this publication may be reproduced, stored in a retrieval system or transmitted in any form or by any means, electronic, mechanical, photocopying, recording, scanning or otherwise, except as expressly permitted by law, without either the prior written permission of the Publisher, or authorization through payment of the appropriate photocopy fee to the Copyright Clearance Center. Requests for permission should be addressed to the Publisher, John Wiley & Sons (Asia) Pte Ltd, 2 Clementi Loop, #02-01, Singapore 129809, tel: 65-64632400, fax: 65-64646912, e-mail: enquiry@wiley.com.sg.

This publication is designed to provide accurate and authoritative information in regard to the subject matter covered. It is sold with the understanding that the publisher is not engaged in rendering professional services. If professional advice or other expert assistance is required, the services of a competent professional person should be sought.

Other Wiley Editorial Offices

John Wiley & Sons, 111 River Street, Hoboken, NJ 07030, USA
John Wiley & Sons, The Atrium Southern Gate, Chichester P019 8SQ, England
John Wiley & Sons (Canada) Ltd, 5353 Dundas Street West, Suite 400, Toronto Ontario M9B 6HB. Canada
John Wiley & Sons Australia Ltd. 42 McDougall Street, Milton, Queensland 4064, Australia
Wiley-VCH, Bosch Strasse 12, D-69469 Weinheim, Germany

Library of Congress Cataloging-in-Publication Data

ISBN-13   978-0-470-82206-7
ISBN-10   0-470-82206-6

Typeset in 12/15 points, Garamond by JC Ruxpin Pte Ltd
Printed in Singapore by Markono Print Media Pte Ltd.
10 9 8 7 6 5 4 3 2 1

CONTENTS

Foreword	vii
Acknowledgements	xi
Chapter 1 Introduction: Women, Growth, and Consumption	1
Chapter 2 Women Consumers in Asia: Know Thy Market	17
Chapter 3 Women Consumers in Affluent Asia: Japan & Korea	43
Chapter 4 Women Consumers in Affluent Asia: Taiwan, Hong Kong & Singapore	71
Chapter 5 Women Consumers in Affluent Asia: Australia	87
Chapter 6 Women Consumers in Emerging Asia: China	101
Chapter 7 Women Consumers in Emerging Asia: India, Malaysia, The Philippines & Thailand	117
Chapter 8 Conclusion: What Do Women Want?	137
Index	159

FOREWORD

The 21st century is the coming of age of Asia as an economic powerhouse. It is also the coming of age of Asian women as an economic force.

The business reality in Asia is that women are the buyers and key decision makers in the purchase of most consumer goods. Increasingly, they are the economic equals of men in the workplace; and they continue to run the household. They are as well as, if not, better educated than their male counterparts, who they also outlive.

A convergence of demographic and economic trends is shaping the consumer market—and it is no exaggeration to say that these new Asian women consumers are "holding up half of the sky."

At MasterCard International, we have watched this evolution and tapped into this market. MasterCard was the first to launch a women's card program in the region, some 16 years ago in Singapore. Women's card programs feature unique benefits that speak to the lifestyle needs of women. MasterCard is committed to this burgeoning market; committed to understanding the lifestyle trends that will be of paramount importance to our female customers and will help us build on our existing brand base through our portfolio of women's card products.

We have seen in many Asia Pacific markets how the impact of population ageing is borne disproportionately by women. Since the coming retirement generation of baby boomers is asset rich, and as women continue to outlive men, a growing proportion of these assets will be controlled by women in their 70s, 80s and 90s. While their retirement resources increase significantly, so will their ability to continue to work part-time as they live longer, healthier and more active lives.

Older women, more active than previous generations, will certainly travel more and stay more involved in recreational activities of all kinds. They will want more personal services, in addition to healthcare, such as women-oriented wealth management and related financial services. On the other hand, the younger singles will have high discretionary spending power as they spend more on themselves, save less and postpone marriage and children.

These lifestyle trends need to be better monitored and better understood.

We have also seen what a growing force women are within the Asian travel market—both in business and leisure travel. These women happen to be the key decision makers when it comes to travel, regardless of who they travel with, who pays for the trip or where they go. Women are fueling an explosive growth within the travel industry, and the industry is just realizing the economic power of women.

As a widely recognized knowledge leader in the Asia Pacific region, MasterCard has devoted extensive resources to developing a deeper understanding of the payments card markets, and the business and economic dynamics that shape this region. The surveys and independent research studies we have undertaken, including the MasterIndex™ of Consumer Confidence, MasterIndex™ of Retail, MasterIndex™ of Travel & Asian Lifestyles, MasterIndex™ of Women's Advancement, are much sought after by analysts, academics and decision makers in financial institutions, government agencies and multinational organizations.

In 2003, MasterCard established the MasterIntelligence Knowledge Panel comprising leading economists and business strategists from across Asia Pacific. The panel, which conducts research and provides insights on the economic and business environment in the region, is headed by Dr. Yuwa Hedrick-Wong, Economic Advisor to MasterCard for Asia Pacific.

Dr. Hedrick-Wong has been instrumental in helping us develop our insights into the fast evolving Asian consumer market. Through a series of MasterCard Insights reports on Asian consumers, and in particular, a study on Asian women consumers launched in 2004, we have demonstrated our commitment to adding value to the understanding of this important market segment with pioneering research. This book is a culmination of some of the research and insights we have sought to bring to businesses across Asia and the world.

André Sekulic
President
MasterCard Asia/Pacific, Middle East & Africa

ACKNOWLEDGEMENT

I would like to acknowledge gratefully the generous support provided by MasterCard International's senior management in Asia/Pacific to make this project possible. Specifically, I would like to thank Mr. André Sekulic, president of MasterCard International Asia/Pacific, South Asia, Middle East and Africa, who lent his personal endorsement to this project; and Ms. Georgette Tan, vice president of MasterCard International Asia/Pacific for her insights and patient guidance in making the book a business oriented and user-friendly one.

I would also like to thank Mr. Ross Burgess and Dr. Clint Laurent, CEO and Chief Technical Officer respectively, of Asian Demographics for their kind permission to use their impressive database, comprehensive and one of a kind in Asia, for much of the analysis used in this book.*

---

*For further information on Asian Demographics, please visit www.asiandemographics.com;
or contact Mr. Ross Burgess at rburgess@asiandemographics.com.

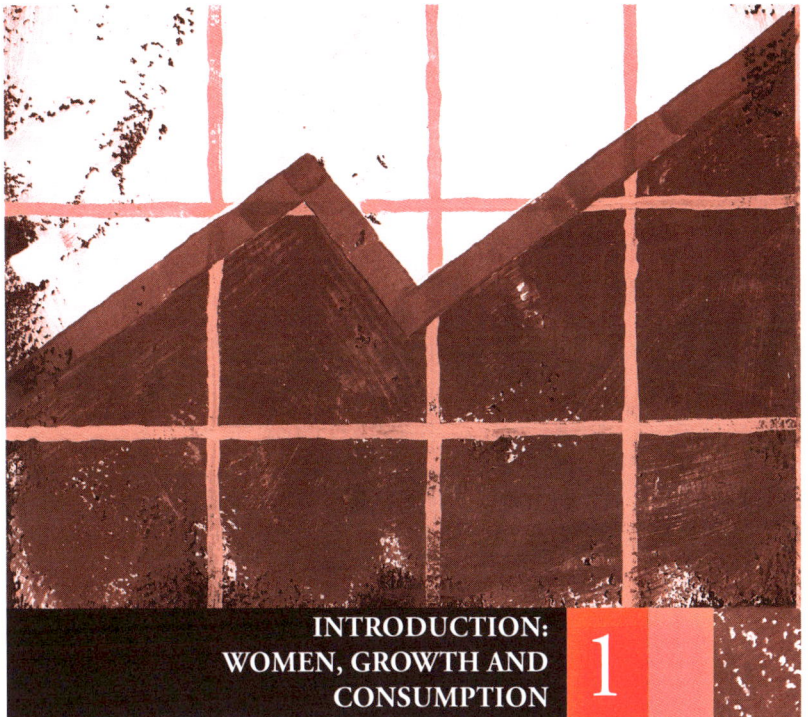

INTRODUCTION: WOMEN, GROWTH AND CONSUMPTION

1

Why are some countries rich and others stuck in poverty? In his book *The Wealth and Poverty of Nations*[1], Harvard professor emeritus David Landes examined five centuries of development to conclude that a country's ability to grow is dependent on a mix of cultural, political and business conditions, such as nurturing entrepreneurs and minimizing market distortion.

He discovered that one of the most important factors in determining economic development was the role of women in society. Landes' observation is simple and unequivocal: If a society wants robust growth, women must contribute fully to the economy and lead full social lives. From the provision of health and education, to job opportunities and career freedom, the wider the scope of women's participation and choices, the better the prospects for rapid and balanced economic growth. From a business perspective, no company can hope to be successful in Asia's consumer markets without a deep understanding of the woman consumers of Asia as they account for a rising share of consumer power as well as increasingly taking center stage in deciding how, when and what to spend.

The evidence is overwhelming. For example, an analysis of economic performance of all countries in the postwar period shows the richest 20% of nations have policies in place to ensure social and economic equality for women, while none of the poorest 20% of nations had such policies.[2] At a basic level, performance is closely related to the general attitudes of the society about the role of women beyond their traditional childbearing role. In many of the poorest countries today, women are expected to be the homemakers and perform many menial tasks and hard labor. In rural West Africa, for example, tradition dictates that women are responsible for fetching water for the family, a daily task that sometimes requires up to three hours of trekking through the bush to reach the closest source of water. Most women in these countries marry early and spend around 15 to 20 years raising children. Under such circumstances, it is near impossible for a woman to pursue a career as raising children takes priority during her most productive working years. In sharp contrast, in developed countries the average woman spends four years in pregnancy and child nursing.[3] She can and does have a career, thus contributing to an economy's productivity and becoming a consumer in her own right, not just for the familial needs.[4]

ADVANCEMENT OF WOMEN IN ASIA

One way to gauge the role of women in society is to look at how many are working, the female unemployment rate and other factors such as the extent to which they have opportunities to exercise their skills and talents, which indicate their overall contribution to economic growth. So, how do Asian women fare from this developmental standpoint? In a global perspective, Asian women rank well in labor force participation, especially in East Asia—Japan, South Korea, China, Taiwan and Hong Kong. For every 100 male workers in the labor force in East Asia in 2003, there were 87 female workers. This is the highest ratio in the world, even higher than the developed OECD countries, where the ratio was 75. Southeast Asia, at 69, is slightly below the OECD ratio. South Asia[5] is significantly lower with a ratio of 47 women to every 100 male workers. (The lowest in the world is the Middle East and Africa with a ratio of just 35.)

Women's participation in the labor force can also be measured by the female unemployment rate. Again, the data show that women workers in East Asia have performed better than women workers in other regions in the world as they have the lowest unemployment rate in the world. At 3% in 2003, it was much lower than the developed world's 7%, the same as is found in Southeast Asia. In other parts of the world, female unemployment is 10% or higher.

But these statistics do not paint the whole picture. In order to better understand the role of women in Asia, a new index was introduced in 2005 by MasterCard International—the MasterIndex of Women's Advancement. This index combines two objective measures—labor force participation and tertiary education level—and the following two subjective measures:

(i) *Managerial position*. The term "managerial position" is intentionally left undefined, and it is up to the respondent to decide whether the employment position is that of a manager or not. A ratio is then derived comparing the percentage of women who believe that they are in managerial positions versus the percentage of men who hold the same belief.

(ii) *Above average income*. Again, "average income" is intentionally left undefined, and the respondent decides whether the income is above average. A ratio is then calculated comparing the percentage of women respondents who believe that their income is above average versus the percentage of men respondents who believe likewise.

How do women in Asia perform according to this index? The results of the first survey, announced in March 2005 (based on 2004 data) are shown in Table 1.1. The overall index value is 68 for the Asia/Pacific region (which includes Australia). This can be interpreted as women's overall performance, averaging the four criteria, is at 68% of that of men. In terms of labor force participation, for every 100 men in the labor force there are 70 women. In tertiary education women perform better: for every 100 men enrolled in tertiary education there are 86 women. Where women perform less well, however, is in the two subjective dimensions of the index. For every 100 men who believe that they are in a managerial position, there are only 61 women who believe so. For every 100 men who believe that they earn above average income, there are only 54 women who believe so.

Table 1.1
MasterIndex of Women Advancement in Asia/Pacific, 2005

Dimension	Index Value
Labor Force Participation	70
Tertiary Education	86
Managerial Position	61
Above Average Income	54
Index Value	68

(MasterCard International Asia/Pacific)

This Asia-wide average, however, conceals considerable variation between individual countries. By comparing the objective criteria against the subjective ones, it is possible to come to some general conclusions about the gap between perceptions and reality.

As is generally true around the world, women often have lower status and salaries in comparison to their male counterparts. By comparing the four criteria one can get a sense of the "gap" between what women have achieved as measured objectively in their participation in the workplace and in higher education; and how they feel about their advancement in spite of what has been achieved.

Table 1.2

MasterIndex of Women Advancement, 2005 Scores

Country	Objective Score (avg)	Subjective Score (avg)	"gap"
Korea	74	17	57
Australia	92	43	49
Singapore	78	45	33
Thailand	107	77	30
China	93	68	27
Indonesia	64	47	17
Philippines	63	55	8
Japan	52	57	5
Taiwan	69	65	4
Malaysia	57	101	44

The results reveal some interesting findings. The countries where there are the largest gaps are in Korea and, most surprising, Australia. The countries with the smallest gaps are Japan, the Philippines and Taiwan. Malaysia is the only country to have a negative gap, where women actually rank themselves higher than their objective criteria would indicate. China, Thailand and Singapore are in the middle. Hence women in the countries with the lowest gaps appear to feel they are given responsibilities and salaries equal to their male counterparts. The data also show other patterns, such as the much lower educational and workforce participation in less developed countries, as one would expect, such as Malaysia,

Indonesia and The Philippines. But, surprisingly, the world's second-largest economy, Japan, also has a low score, a sign of that country's continuing underutilization of its female population. Meanwhile Thailand and China score relatively high, an encouraging sign for their "growth" prospects.

The objective achievement in labor force participation and education does not always produce strong positive self-perception as indicated by the sometimes surprisingly large "gap" between the objective and subjective scores. The subjective perception women have of themselves is astoundingly modest in view of the highly significant role they will have in shaping the consumer markets of Asia in the future, as will be shown in the subsequent chapters in this book.

CONSUMER SOVEREIGNTY

Rising domestic consumption will play an increasingly important role in the future of Asian economies. A sustained rise in private consumption as the new locomotive of economic growth in Asia in the coming years is not only a certainty, but a prospect welcomed by governments and businesses alike. The same could not be said, however, less than half a dozen years ago. The conventional wisdom was savings and investments are good, consumption is at best to be kept moderate; and consumption of "luxuries" should be actively discouraged by punitive taxes and import tariffs. Several decades of export-led success in East and Southeast Asia had entrenched the idea that export-oriented industries need to be supported (and subsidized if necessary) by high domestic savings and investment. And the best way to do that is to make sure that the working people in Asia are prodigious savers but frugal consumers.

This formula worked for many years, resulting in Asian growth rates lifting millions out of poverty and making the region the economic dynamo it is today. But now Asia is reaching a turning point as economies mature. Today, the domestic consumer markets in Asia are typically underdeveloped. This is reflected in the much lower levels of GDP being accounted for by private domestic consumption in Asia when compared to developed countries. For most high-income Western countries, domestic consumption is half or more of the economy and in the US it is a whopping 68% of GDP. As a result, growth in the US economy is largely driven by its domestic sector—as long as Americans feel good and open up their wallets, their economy grows.

Table 1.3
Domestic Consumption as Percentage of GDP*

US	68
Taiwan	63
Korea	56
Japan	55
Malaysia	50
Singapore	46
China	46

*2001-2004 average, source: World Bank

In a historical perspective, the "consumption revolution" is not only needed in Asia as a new growth locomotive, but it is also critically important for creating more balanced and therefore sustainable growth. It is a radical and fundamental departure from the policies and ideologies of the past. Consumption is not some frivolous activity as some die-hard members of the old guard still maintain. Instead, it plays a profound role in value creation, with far-reaching implications.

When consumers call the shots, economies thrive. Consumption is at the heart of the value creation process. It is central to efficient resource allocation and productivity. Production of any good or service is meaningless if the final output is not something that consumers want to buy or use. Consider a block of ice. What is its value? Imagine trying to determine the price of ice by adding up the cost of production, without taking into account where it is to be sold. The same block of ice commands vastly different prices between the Sahara Desert and northern Alaska. What is the difference? The consumer. Consumers value ice when in the Sahara but it is worthless to Eskimos. The production technology for making ice is the same, the water molecules in the ice are the same. Its value changes depending on the consumer.

When consumers are allowed to choose freely, their preferences are the signals that producers must heed. Thus they will be able to determine what to invest and how much to invest in order to have the right kinds and levels of product to make a profit. And, as consumer preferences shift, producers must follow suit if they are to stay in business. So consumption determines value. And consumers "vote" with their wallets on a daily basis in the greatest democracy on earth—the multi-participant market.

BUILD IT AND THEY WILL BUY?

This approach turns the traditional Asian model on its head. In East Asia, "strategic" industries were identified by the government because they were seen as being in the promising export-led sector. They were supported by generous and usually state-subsidized loans and grants, and protected by tariffs and otherwise coddled. This artificial "abundance" of capital eventually led to business follies of gigantic proportions. In Korea, the large conglomerates known as *chaebols* were thought to be too big to fail, and they pursued single-mindedly an expansion of their market shares at home and overseas without paying heed to profitability. By the mid-1990s, just before the onset of the 1997 financial crisis, their returns on investment were negative. They usually had huge levels of debt because capital was virtually free for them.

Typical of this process was a decision by Kun-Hee Lee, the legendary founder of Samsung, the largest Korean *chaebol*, to make Samsung cars, at a time when the industry was suffering from a severe global overcapacity and the domestic Korean market was also saturated by the likes of Hyundai and others. Never mind that Samsung had no expertise in the car business. In reply to critics, Lee simply said, "Samsung could not fail." In other words, what consumers may think was of no consequence to Samsung—the assumption was what Samsung produces, consumers buy.

Similar follies were committed in Japan, on an even bigger scale. In the aftermath of the burst of the bubble economy in the early 1990s, companies were asked by senior bureaucrats not to downsize and not to cut back on production. In other words, they were asked to continue business as usual, pretending nothing had happened. Banks were urged to extend new loans to these companies to keep them afloat even as their losses were mounting. The result was a prolonged economic stagnation lasting through the 1990s and into the early 2000s. A consumer-focused approach would have allowed changing consumer choices to drive changes in business practice; even if it entailed business failures and bankruptcies. New and more viable businesses would have been created, which would in turn create new employment and income. Instead, Japan suffered from deflation, the crippling of the entire banking sector, high unemployment and low income. The government now has the highest level of public debt seen in developed countries. It is only in the last few years that Junichiro Koizumi, the prime minister who staked his job on economic reform, has started slowly to turn things around.

No other systems, however, can top central planning when it comes to ignoring the consumer. As seen in the cost in human lives and suffering, the follies committed by central planning of the communist authorities in China were arguably far more severe. The absurd extreme of this practice is steel production in the 1950s during the "Great Leap Forward" program. Lacking production capacity, the government decided that, analogous to the "people's war" concept, every village should produce its share of steel and thus contribute to the national effort. A massive campaign was launched and villages in China were instructed to build "backyard" furnaces to make steel. Not surprisingly many villages did not have their own supply of iron ore, so village leaders started to collect cast iron household utensils, window and door frames in public buildings, even priceless antique gates and ceremonial bells in ancestral shrines, and melted them down as raw materials for the village furnace to make steel. Equally unsurprising the quality of "steel" produced was utterly substandard. They were lumps of misshapen metal that could not be used for anything. Thus, useful items were destroyed to make a useless product, which was then proudly reported to the central government in terms of tons of "steel" produced. The central government duly added up the tonnage, then reported to the whole country that the campaign was successful and socialism had triumphed once again.[6]

Ironically, the real "Great Leap Forward" in China was ignited only in the late 1990s when the consumption revolution got underway. When consumers were given the freedom to buy what they wanted and businesses were given the freedom to respond, China's entrepreneurial private companies thrived while the state-run centrally planned factories stagnated.

The consumption revolution, however, can never be complete without the full participation of women. It also follows that without women's full participation, the process of value creation in an economy will be less successful. The changing role of women in work and in their private lives is one of the most underappreciated in the region. As the household is the center of consumption, women can have a huge influence on consumption habits. In this regard, women really are holding up half of the sky. And, in the coming years, no business can hope to be successful in Asia's consumer markets without a deep understanding of the woman consumer of Asia.

A GENERATIONAL PERSPECTIVE

The pace of change in Asia, both in terms of economic growth and social transformation, has been nothing less than breathtaking in the past half century. Japan rose from postwar devastation to become the second largest economy in the world. Singapore leapt from a third-world trading post to a sparkling first-world city state within one generation. China threw away its centrally planned economy to champion globalization. Thailand, once a major recipient of foreign aid, is now a donor country providing foreign aid to other poor countries. India, once written off as stuck in the "Hindu rate of [slow] growth", is now limbering up and getting in shape, with economic reform, to play in the global major league.

As a result of such fast change, the attitude and behavior of women consumers in Asia cannot be fully understood without taking into account the specific historical contexts in which the different women consumer age groups grew up. In this regard, an analysis of their generation's background is useful. Introducing generational groupings allows a focus on the broader cultural and socioeconomic contexts which influence life experiences and behavioral patterns. How economic, political and social reconstruction in the 1950s shaped Japan's war generation may explain the resilience and sense of tenacity of Japanese women in their 60s. The technological revolution of the 1990s was a significant driver in many countries, but particularly in Korea, where women in their 20s are among the most tech-savvy in the world. It is not surprising that Korean women are some of the most avid online shoppers and cell phone users. The Chinese Cultural Revolution of the 1960s and 1970s impacted significantly on women who lived through those turbulent years and left its imprints on their general attitude toward their lives today and how they behave as consumers.

But generations are also global phenomena. While the current demarcations of generations are admittedly Western-centric, they can nonetheless enhance understanding of generational changes, especially in terms of their impact on Asian women.

The first to consider is the so-called Silent Generation (aged 59 to 79). Its members represent a "silent" generation because they grew up in an era when the championing of women's rights and equal treatment had yet to come; and women still lacked a public voice. In much of Asia, they are a generation born into a colonial world. The older among them experienced the Second World War and all of them lived through the subsequent struggles for independence, the national fervor, and are now enjoying relatively high disposable net worth in retirement, the fruits of thrifty savings and gains made during the peak period of Asia's economic miracle. Japanese women in this generation, for example, are knowledgeable and adventurous travelers.

Baby boomers (aged 40 to 58) are so named because through their sheer numbers, they created an unprecedented, global, human population wave. Many female baby boomers in Asia are settled in careers and marriages, and are busy mothers. They are the first generation to have been molded by the post-independence nationalism of the 1960s. They are also the first female beneficiaries of improving educational and career opportunities for women. They are pathfinders, and grew up in a world profoundly different from their mothers' generation. Many developed a taste for travel during their 20s, when many worked and also postponed marriage to enjoy an independent lifestyle. Now either single and settled in careers, or married with families, this generation of women in Asia are careful and discerning consumers.

Generation X (aged 24 to 39) —also called the "me generation" —are really hitting their stride today. Most are out of school and into careers. Generation X women in Asia span the life stages of "single women," "married with no children" and, for some, in response to pressures, "women with children." In the West, defining moments for female Generation Xers revolve around the profound changes in child-rearing which occurred in the 1980s, when dual incomes, higher divorce rates, and remarriages became more common. To a similar extent the same patterns can be found in Asia, especially among the "young singles."

Generation Y (aged 4 to 23) —also called the Millennium Generation—are still in school, or taking their initial steps on career paths. For the majority, marriage is still in the future, given the trend toward later marriage in Asia. Certainly a defining element of this generation is its tech-savviness. Generation Yers surf the internet on wireless broadband and their mobile phones have become an almost organic appendage. Particularly in Asia, use of SMS is a way of life for this generation. This tech-savviness, combined with more free time and higher disposable incomes makes them an important segment in the consumer market.

The biggest advantage to thinking in generational terms is that it allows us to track the same group of women through the various stages of their lives. Take for example, the famous Japanese Office Ladies. They were wooed by the luxury brands and the travel industry in the 1990s not only because of their high disposable incomes, their penchant to spend lavishly on branded goods, but most importantly for their sense of adventure—pioneering new holiday destinations, such as beach holidays in Bali, Langkawi and Phuket.

Ten years on, where is this pioneering group of Japanese Office Ladies? They are the mainstays of Generation X. This may help to explain why so many Japanese women in their 30s are still keen shoppers and travelers. Even though they have grown into their 30s, and some have married and had children, they have not lost their passion for shopping and travel. In contrast, those who are still bent on cultivating the Office Ladies in Japan today may also be off the mark. After 10 years of economic stagnation, today's Japanese female 20-somethings (Generation Y) are not taking to the skies as exuberantly as their "elder sisters," as confirmed by statistics. The women of the "me generation" behave very differently as consumers from those not even a decade older than they are.

How different generations interact could also affect their consumption behavior. For example, there is the trend toward mother-daughter, and mother-daughter plus granddaughter travel in Asia, especially in Japan. This trend is an interesting extension of family travel. High disposable incomes of one generation combined with travel-savvy planning skills of another generation are sending these intergenerational family teams all over Asia to shop, visit spas and stay at luxury resorts.

In Japan, it is women in their 60s and older, retirees with high disposable incomes, who are the chief funding sources for these intergenerational holidays. Since the late 1990s, Japanese women in their 30s, particularly those who are still single, travel more frequently due to the generosity of their parents. In Japan, grandmothers also appear to be indulging the youngest generation. These doting grandparents, with high savings and accumulated assets, can treat their working daughters so that they and their husbands can have a well-deserved break from work and children. A similar pattern can be observed in China where young adults who are the single child of the family benefit from two sets of dotting grandparents. Anecdotal evidence suggests that this may indeed be an emerging trend in the rest of Asia. These generation-related issues are a rich source of insights in understanding the woman consumer in Asia as she evolves through precisely defined "lifecycle stages."

WOMEN CONSUMERS IN ASIA: KNOW THY MARKET 2

Women in the key markets in Asia Pacific[1] number over 1.3 billion, a number which will reach 1.5 billion by 2014. As a consumer market, it is not only the size of the female population that is important, but also the households in which they live. Households are the primary units of consumption. A household with many children usually means a busy mother with little spare cash or extra time to spend outside the family. On the other hand, a household with the same income but with a single child has more money to go around after taking care of the necessities. A household consisting of a young couple with no plan for children can devote its disposable income to themselves. An elderly couple living on their own, healthy and with substantial net assets, are likely to be active and discerning consumers. Thus companies need to determine not just what type of women they want to market to but also what kind of household.

Households can be divided into four broad segments: the young, the middle aged married, empty nesters, and the elderly. Then each of these groups can be split into two stages (with the exception of the first group, which has three stages). Some women may pass through all four segments as the family situation changes.

YOUNG HOUSEHOLDS

The three lifecycle stages of the young household are:

- Young single: Under 35 years old and with no children, young singles in Asia represent a new lifestyle trend, as more of them opt to stay single or postpone marriage. The young singles, who are largely urban based, are strongly correlated with higher levels of education and have professional careers. This group have significant disposable incomes, and their consumption is mostly on discretionary items as opposed to basic necessities. Many are dating, which means frequent dining out and many social activities. Being young and technologically savvy, they are also adventurous consumers and more willing to try new services and products. It is no surprise that young singles are brand conscious, with fast-moving tastes, and are the first to adopt new trends.

- Young married: Married with no children and under 35 years old, young marrieds may or may not be planning to have children. Those planning to have children are likely to be high savers for their future families, whereas those who do not plan to have children are likely to behave like young singles.

- Young married with young child: These couples, under 39 and with a child under 10, have lives that are largely dominated by child-rearing needs. The well-being of the child typically takes priority over other concerns. In many countries in Asia, however, the extended family unit still remains intact, and grandparents and close relatives often contribute to the labor and expenses of bringing up the child, which allows the couple to have both time and money to continue to enjoy active social lives.

MIDDLE AGED MARRIED

The segment of middle aged and married households consists of one lifecycle stages: those married and under 39 years old with young children, and those who are over 39 years old with children.

- Middle aged under 39 with children: With children between the ages of 11 and 20, household expenditures are heavily skewed toward the provision of schooling, healthcare and other needs of the children. For urban middle class families in this stage, there is also the need to save for the children's university education expenses. Disposable income tends to be quite low for these households after rent or mortgage payment, savings and regular family-related expenses.

EMPTY NESTERS

The empty nester households have two lifecycle stages:

- Working age empty nester: These are couples between 40 and 64 years old with no dependent children at home. Either both are working, or one works (usually the male), and the other stays home (usually the female). Many of these households have finished their mortgage payments, and enjoy relatively high disposable incomes.

- Working age single: Either unmarried or widowed, they are between 40 and 64 years old. Their children, should they have any, have left home or are no longer dependent on them, so they are also empty nesters. Again, these are people with significant disposable incomes who have no one to spend money on but themselves.

ELDERLY HOUSEHOLDS

Finally, the elderly households segment is also comprised of two lifecycle stages:

- Retired empty nester: They are married, over 64, retired with no dependent children. As life expectancy continues to rise, the health status of the elderly is also improving. Those who are 65 and above today are expected to live the longest, the healthiest and the most active lives in history. The retired empty nesters in Asia are also expected to have an active lifestyle in the coming decades.

- Retired old single: Either unmarried or widowed, over 64, retired, these people are mortgage-free and living on their own. Similar to the retired empty nesters, their life expectancy and health status are expected to be long and robust. For the widows in these households, they are the first generation in Asia to benefit from their husbands' life insurance. These elderly women therefore have the financial wherewithal to pursue an active lifestyle and afford quality healthcare if needed.

Having identified the nine different lifecycle stages in Asia, let's turn to conditions within individual countries and how demographics will shape the evolution of the women consumers in each one.

A NEW GRAY MARKET

Two broad trends are at work, both are turning traditional images of Asia on their heads: The first is that, on average, Asia's populations are getting older; the second is that population growth is slowing across the region. These two trends reinforce each other and are in contrast to most of the postwar decades when Asia had fast-growing and young populations. The "graying" in the Western world is spreading to Asia. In fact, the fastest-growing household segment across Asia will be the elderly, increasing 5.5% on average in the 12 countries surveyed below (with one exception, India, where it is the second fastest-growing segment after empty nesters).

Table 2.1
Ageing Asia

	Average age of population	
Country	2004	2024
Australia	37	41
China	34	44
Hong Kong	38	47
India	28	33
Indonesia	28	34
Japan	42	48
Korea	34	43
Malaysia	27	33
Philippines	26	30
Singapore	34	39
Taiwan	34	41
Thailand	32	40

(Asian Demographics)

The most dramatic example is Asia's largest economy, Japan. Most of us know that Japan's baby boomers are turning it into the "oldest" country in the world. Today, the average age in Japan is 42 and will rise to 48 in 2024. Hong Kong will have the second oldest population in Asia by 2024, followed by China. While all the major countries of Asia will see a rise in the average age, the greatest shift is happening in East Asia, most significantly in China, with its huge population.

ASIA'S SLOWDOWN: SAYONARA MALTHUS

Apart from being the oldest in Asia, Japan's population will also be the first to shrink in Asia. In the coming decade, it is expected to shrink 0.1% per year, and shrink even faster in the decade after that. As shown in Table 2.2, population growth is slowing across the entire region. Only three countries will have growth at 1.5% or above in Asia: Malaysia, the Philippines and India.

Table 2.2
Slowing Population Growth

	Average annual rate of growth	
Country	1994 - 2004	2004 – 2014
Japan	0.2%	-0.1%
China	0.8%	0.2%
Korea	0.8%	0.4%
Thailand	0.7%	0.4%
Taiwan	0.8%	0.5%
Hong Kong SAR	1.5%	0.7%
Indonesia	1.0%	0.7%
Australia	0.8%	0.7%
Singapore	1.6%	1.2%
India	1.9%	1.5%
Philippines	2.2%	1.6%
Malaysia	2.5%	1.8%

(Asian Demographics)

Another broad trend across Asia is that women are opting to stay single, or if they marry, to have children at a later age or not at all. Hence in Asian societies, the numbers of single women, women with smaller or no families and the elderly are growing.

JAPAN

Now let's combine the demographic trends with the household segments described above. Japan shows a dramatic rise in one particular class of women: elderly women. They will be healthier, wealthier and live longer than ever before, all of which signals the rise of a major new market in the country. This trend is generally true across Asia.

In Japan, the young households segment will decline by an average of 1% per year in the next decade. In contrast, the women classified as empty nesters or elderly will rise by nearly 50% by 2014 to a combined total of 32 million.

Table 2.3

JAPAN: Women Population (Individuals)

JAPAN (000)	2004	2014	Av. Annual Growth Rate
Young Households	20752.6	17953.0	-1.35%
Middle Aged Households With children	7744.8	8051.8	0.40%
Empty nesters (Working)	14100.0	13607.3	-0.35%
Elderly Households (Retired)	14071.6	18117.5	2.88%

(MasterCard Asia/Pacific, Asian Demographics)

Important changes in Japanese society are revealed by Chart 2.1. For one, there will be more elderly women than men in Japan as women outlive men by about 10 years. Elderly women in Japan as a percentage of the total women population will also increase. In 2004, for example, women over 65 years old accounted for 22% of the total women population in Japan. By 2014, it is expected that they will account for an astonishing 28%—the highest in Asia. Japan will therefore have proportionally more elderly people, as well as proportionally more women among the elderly, than any other country in Asia.

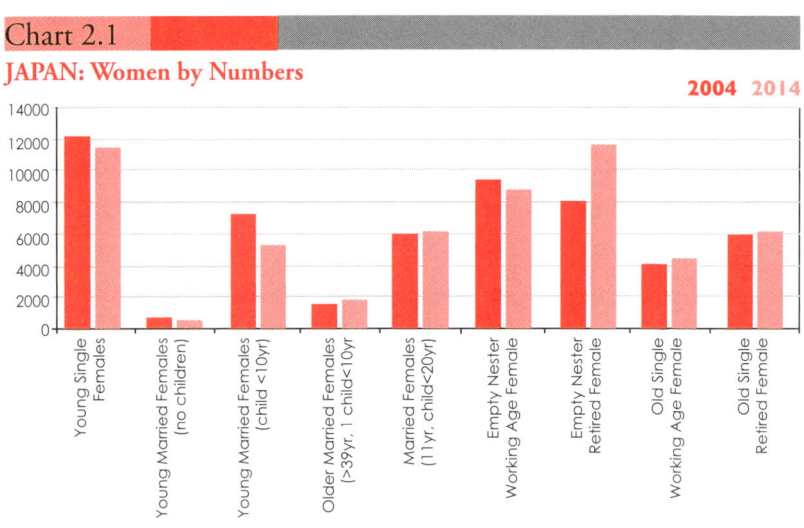

(Asian Demographics)

Take for example Japan's centenarians, people who are over 100 years old. The number of centenarians in Japan stood at 25,606 at the end of September 2005. An impressive 85% of them were women. They are the tip of a huge iceberg of elderly women consumers that prefer different products and services from their young peers. A whole new range of new business opportunities is opening up, catering to the elderly women consumers of Japan. The women consumer market in Japan will be powerfully shaped by these demographic trends in the next decade.

KOREA

Korea's population is also ageing fast. In 2004, the average age of all Koreans was 34. By 2014, it will be 43, a jump of one year in average age for almost every chronological year. The changing nature of the Korean female population by the four household segments is summarized in Table 2.4. While the young households will shrink by 1% per year in the next decade, the empty nesters will grow strongly by 3% per year. The elderly households segment will grow at an even higher rate of 5%.

Table 2.4

KOREA: Women Population (Individuals)

KOREA (000)	2004	2014	Av. Annual Growth Rate
Young Households	9523.7	8366.3	-1.22%
Middle Aged Households with Children	3237.5	3776.9	1.67%
Empty Nesters (working)	4146.6	5419.9	3.07%
Elderly Households (retired)	2417.0	3533.1	4.62%

(MasterCard Asia/Pacific, Asian Demographics)

The changing size of the nine lifecycle stages in the women population is shown in Chart 2.2. In spite of the expected shrinkage of the young households segment at the rate of 1.3% decline per year in the next decade, the size of the young singles is expected to buck this trend and actually increase. Again, this trend is a reflection of changing lifestyles as more young Koreans opt to stay single which more than compensates for the decline in the overall size of the young households segment. The empty nesters and elderly households segments are all expected to increase in size.

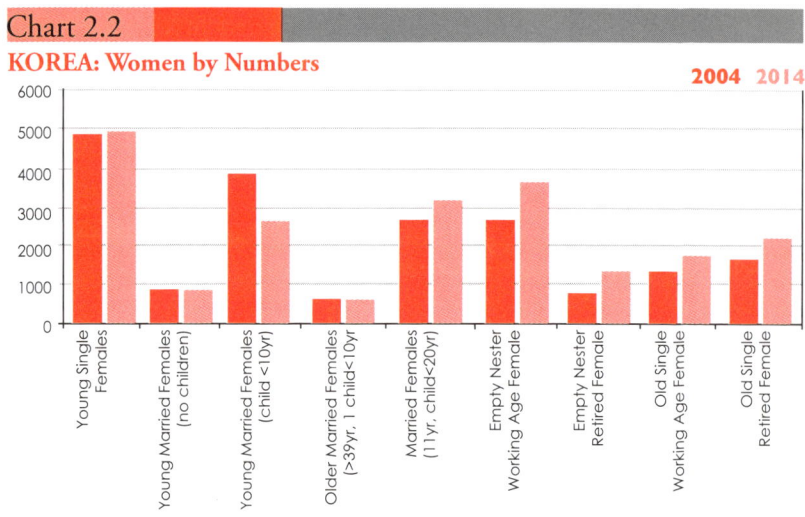

(Asian Demographics)

Elderly women in Korea are also expected to become more dominant as a percentage of the total women population. In 2004, women 65 years old and above accounted for 10% of all women. By 2014, it will be 14%.

HONG KONG

Hong Kong's population is the second oldest in Asia after Japan. And it is expected to grow only very slowly in the next decade at an average rate of 0.7% per year. In the coming decade, the young households segment will decline by 1% per year, whereas the other three segments will gain. The empty nesters and the elderly households segments are expected to grow impressively by 6% and 5% respectively. By 2014, the combined population size of these two segments will be about 1.6 million, only slightly smaller than the combined young households and middle aged married segments of 1.9 million. Most of these elderly women in Hong Kong are relatively well educated, and many have been active in the business world as professionals and executives. The best of them embody high quality human capital that is much needed in Hong Kong's increasingly knowledge intensive economy. To be able to create opportunities for them to be engaged in productive roles in society even in their 60s and early 70s would effectively mitigate the impact of the slowdown in the growth of the workforce. This shift therefore has enormous implications for the Hong Kong economy, especially for its focus on being a regional business hub.

Table 2.5
HONG KONG: Women Population (Individuals)

HONG KONG (000)	2004	2014	Av. Annual Growth Rate
Young Households	1367.9	1212.8	-1.13%
Middle Aged Households with Children	648.1	670.7	0.35%
Empty Nesters (working)	589.6	955.9	6.21%
Elderly Households (retired)	436.0	633.6	4.53%

(MasterCard Asia/Pacific, Asian Demographics)

The specific lifecycle stages among women in Hong Kong is shown in Chart 2.3. Similar to the situation in Korea, the number of young singles will grow even though the overall size of the young households segment will be shrinking. Lifecycle stages are expected to expand rapidly for the empty nesters and elderly households segments. There will also be more elderly women in Hong Kong in the coming decade. In 2004, women 65 years and above accounted for 12% of the total women population. By 2014, it will rise to 16%.

Chart 2.3
HONG KONG: Women by Numbers

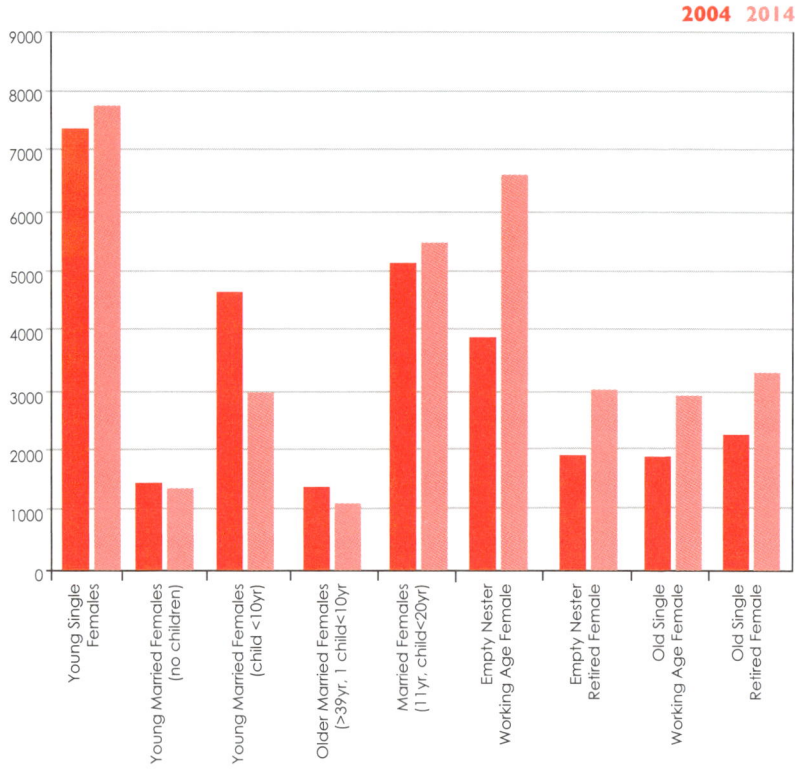

(Asian Demographics)

TAIWAN

Consistent with the pattern in East Asia, Taiwan's population is also ageing fast. In 2004, the average age in Taiwan was 34, and by 2014 it will be 41. The population will grow at a slow rate of some 0.5% per year in the coming decade. The young households segment in Taiwan's women population will shrink by 1% per year in the next decade, while the other three segments will grow by 2%, 3% and 5% per year respectively.

Table 2.6
TAIWAN: Women Population (Individuals)

TAIWAN (000)	2004	2014	Av. Annual Growth Rate
Young Households	4535.9	4163.3	-0.82%
Middle Aged Households with Children	1549.0	1854.3	1.97%
Empty Nesters (working)	1898.6	2378.0	2.53%
Elderly Households (retired)	1038.9	1582.1	5.23%

(MasterCard Asia/Pacific, Asian Demographics)

The number of young women singles in Taiwan, just as in Korea and Hong Kong, will grow in spite of the overall decline of the young households segment, due to changing lifestyles. Both the young marrieds with no children segment and the young marrieds with a child under 10 group will shrink in size, reflecting young Taiwanese women's growing reluctance to have children.

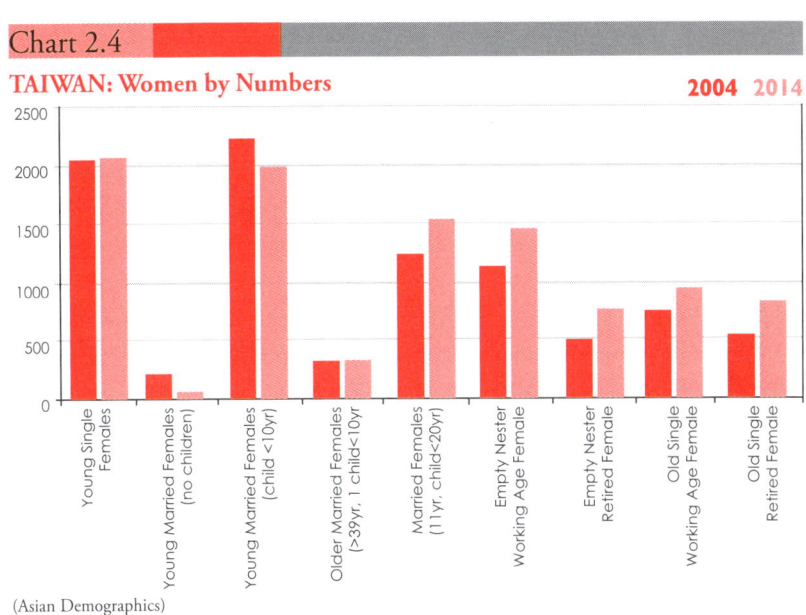

Chart 2.4
TAIWAN: Women by Numbers   2004 2014

(Asian Demographics)

The number of elderly women in Taiwan will also grow proportionally. In 2004, women over 65 years old accounted for 9% of the total women population. This figure is expected to rise to 13% by 2014.

SINGAPORE

Singapore's population is also ageing, from an average of 34 years in 2004 to 41 years in 2014. The population will continue to grow, albeit at a slower rate of 1.2% per year in the next decade. Unlike the other East Asian countries, Singapore's women population will expand in all the four broad segments, including the young households segment. The fastest rate of growth will be found in the elderly households segment at an astonishing annual rate of 7%, followed by the empty nesters at 4%. The young households and middle aged with children segments are expected to grow at 0.6% and 0.5% per year respectively.

Table 2.7
SINGAPORE: Women Population (Individuals)

SINGAPORE (000)	2004	2014	Av. Annual Growth Rate
Young households	586.9	619.0	0.55%
Middle Aged Households with Children	264.7	278.5	0.52%
Empty nesters (Working)	381.2	517.8	3.58%
Elderly households (Retired)	112.4	195.0	7.34%

(MasterCard Asia/Pacific, Asian Demographics)

The changing size of the lifecycle stages is shown in Chart 2.5. With the exception of the young married with a child under 10, all the lifecycle stages are expected to grow in the coming decade.

Women over 65 years old accounted for 7% of the total women population in 2004 in Singapore. This percentage is expected to rise to 10% in 2014.

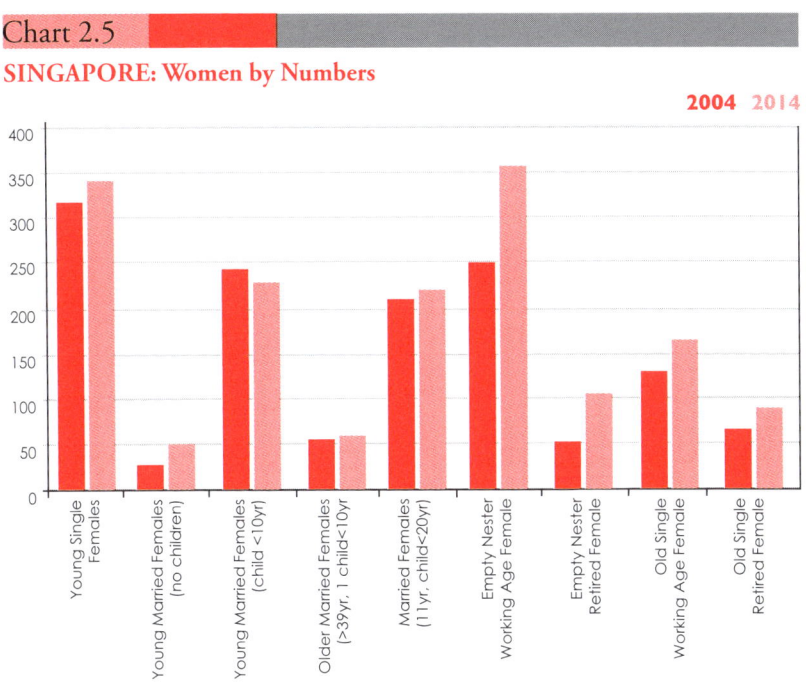

(Asian Demographics)

CHINA

Due to the "One Child" policy, introduced in 1978, China's population growth has slowed significantly in the past two decades. The average age of the Chinese population in 2004 was 33, but will rise to 44 in 2014, an increase in average age that is faster than chronological years (i.e., 11 years increase in just a decade). The population growth rate, on the other hand, will slow to an average of 0.2% per year in the next decade. The population in China is projected to begin shrinking after 2014, thus joining Japan as a shrinking nation.

The women population in the young households and middle aged segments will decline by 1.8% and 0.2% per year respectively in the coming years. In contrast, the empty nesters and elderly households segments will grow strongly by 6% and 4% respectively. By 2014, there will be a combined 238 million women in the empty nesters and elderly households segments, representing a huge new consumer market. Laid against the background of the fast growth of China's economy, this segment of China's women's market is set to become more attractive in the future, especially for the empty nesters who are, by definition, households without economically dependent children at home. Many of these households will spend their rising disposable income either on themselves or on their precious grandchildren. Many of these grandchildren are the single child in the family, hence with two sets of grandparents competing to spend and dote on them.

Table 2.8
CHINA: Women Population (Individuals)

CHINA (000)	2004	2014	Av. Annual Growth Rate
Young Households	240954.6	197712.6	-1.79%
Middle Aged Households with Children	115474.4	118094.4	0.23%
Empty Nesters (working)	97939.3	158469.1	6.18%
Elderly Households (retired)	58528.1	79554.3	3.59%

(MasterCard Asia/Pacific, Asian Demographics)

Chart 2.6 shows the changing size of the women population in the different lifecycle stages. The number of young singles will shrink so will the number of young marrieds with a child under 10 and middle aged marrieds with children between 10 and 20. But the young marrieds with no child will grow, again, a clear reflection of a changing lifestyle of young people opting to remain single. All the older lifecycle stages will grow in size.

Chart 2.6
CHINA: Women by Numbers

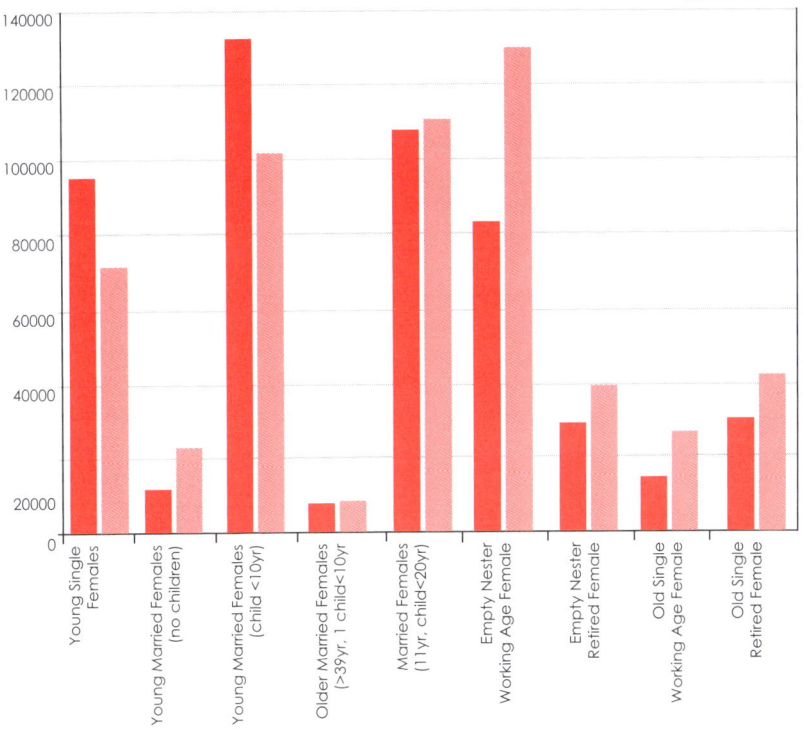

(Asian Demographics)

Older women will also increase their presence in the total women population in China. In 2004, women over 65 years old accounted for 10% of the total women population. It will rise to 13% in 2014.

AUSTRALIA

Australia's population is among the fastest ageing. In 2004, the average age of all Australians was 37. By 2014 it will be 41. Meantime, the population will only grow by about 0.7% per year in the coming decade. The women population is expected to increase in all the four broad segments. The fastest-growing is the elderly households segment at 3% per year, followed by the middle aged with children households at 2% and the empty nesters at 1%. The young households segment has the lowest growth rate at 0.03% per year. By 2014, the combined women population of the empty nesters and elderly households segments will be 3.5 million.

Table 2.9
AUSTRALIA: Women Population (Individuals)

AUSTRALIA (000)	2004	2014	Av. Annual Growth Rate
Young Households	3430.2	3440.6	0.03%
Middle Aged Households with Children	1342.7	1584.3	1.80%
Empty Nesters (working)	1606.8	1835.9	1.43%
Elderly Households (retired)	1351.2	1707.1	2.63%

(MasterCard Asia/Pacific, Asian Demographics)

Chart 2.7 shows that all lifecycle stages are expected to increase in size in the next decade, with the exception of the young marrieds with a child under 10. This reluctance of young women to have children is consistent with the gradual slowdown of Australia's population growth. Older women will increase their share in the overall women population quite dramatically. In 2004, women aged 65 years or older accounted for only 4% of the total women population. By 2014, it will increase to an impressive 13%.

Chart 2.7
AUSTRALIA: Women by Numbers

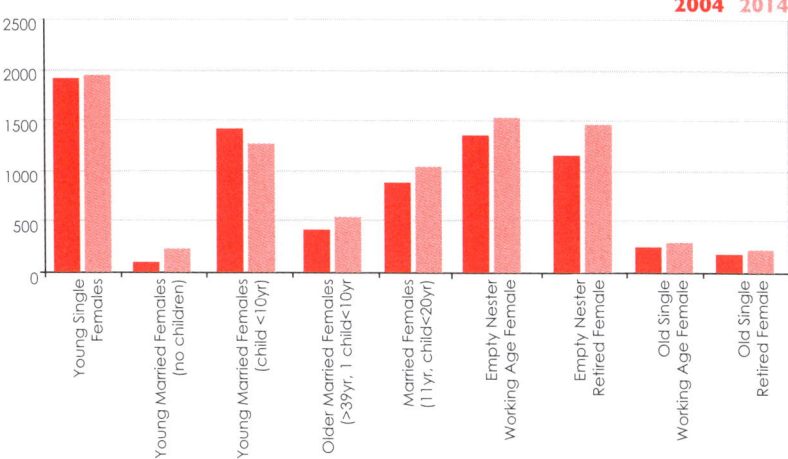

(Asian Demographics)

THAILAND

Thailand has the oldest population among middle income emerging Asia. In 2004, the average age of the Thai population was 32. It is expected to rise to 40 by 2014. Population growth is also slowing significantly from an annual average of 0.7% in the past decade to 0.4% in the next decade.

Table 2.10
THAILAND: Women Population (Individuals)

THAILAND (000)	2004	2014	Av. Annual Growth Rate
Young Households	12948.1	11458.9	-1.15%
Middle Aged Households with Children	5218.1	5653.9	0.84%
Empty Nesters (working)	4306.7	6480.6	5.05%
Elderly Households (retired)	2418.8	3931.6	6.25%

(MasterCard Asia/Pacific, Asian Demographics)

The Thai women population in the young households segment will decline by 1% per year in the next decade. The other segments, the middle aged with children, empty nesters and elderly households, will grow by 1%, 5% and 6% per year respectively. The elderly households growth of 6% per year is especially impressive. By 2014, there will be 10 million Thai women in the empty nesters and elderly households segments. In terms of the specific lifecycle stages, the young marrieds without a child will grow slightly, while both the young singles and marrieds with a child under 10 will decline. All other lifecycle stages will see strong growth.

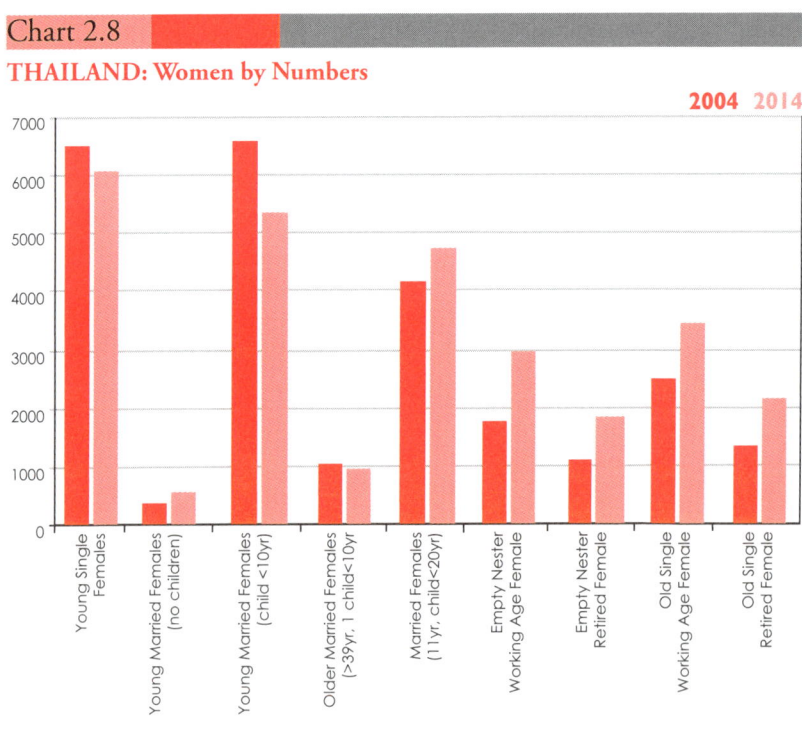

Chart 2.8

THAILAND: Women by Numbers

(Asian Demographics)

The percentage of women over 65 years old in Thailand is extraordinarily high. In 2004, 16% of all Thai women were over the age of 65. By 2014, 24% of them will be over 65 years old, making

Thailand second only to Japan in terms of the size of the elderly as a percentage of the total female population.

MALAYSIA

Malaysia has one of the youngest populations in Asia. In 2004 the average age of Malaysians was 27, and by 2014 it will be only 33. Population growth will remain strong at 2% per year in the next decade.

All four segments of the women population will grow in the next decade. The elderly households segment will have the highest growth at 8% per year, followed by the empty nesters and middle aged with children segments, both at 3% per year. The young households segment, the slowest growing, will still be expanding by 2% per year.

Table 2.11
MALAYSIA: Women Population (Individuals)

MALAYSIA (000)	2004	2014	Av. Annual Growth Rate
Young Households	5374.4	6202.3	1.54%
Middle Aged Households with Children	1902.3	2483.0	3.05%
Empty Nesters (working)	878.2	1178.7	3.42%
Elderly Households (retired)	485.8	882.9	8.17%

(MasterCard Asia/Pacific, Asian Demographics)

The changing size of the specific lifecycle stages is shown in Chart 2.9. All are expected to expand over the next decade. Malaysian women will remain relatively young. In 2004, only 4% of women in Malaysia were over 65 years old. By 2014, this will rise to just 6%.

Chart 2.9
MALAYSIAN: Women by Numbers

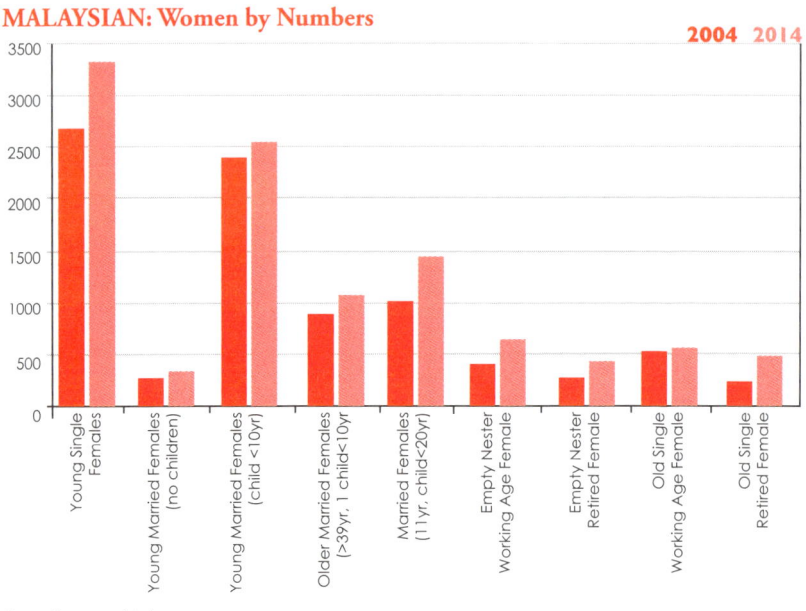

(Asian Demographics)

THE PHILIPPINES

The Philippines has the youngest population in Asia. In 2004, the average age of the Philippine population was only 26, and will rise to a mere 30 in 10 years' time. Its population will also continue to be one of the fastest growing. The average annual rate of growth in the coming decade is expected to be 2%.

Given the overall population's youth and high growth rates, all four women population segments will be expanding. The fastest growing segment will be the elderly household segment at 5% per year, albeit from a very small base. While the young households segment will be growing at only 2% per year, it was the largest segment at 17 million in 2004, and projected to increase to 20 million in 2014. It is bigger than the other three segments combined. Young women will continue to dominate in terms of sheer size in the Philippines.

Table 2.12
THE PHILIPPINES: Women Population (Individuals)

THE PHILIPPINES (000)	2004	2014	Av. Annual Growth Rate
Young Households	16983.9	19996.9	1.77%
Middle Aged Households with Children	5247.1	6957.8	3.26%
Empty Nesters (working)	2446.9	3567.0	4.58%
Elderly Households (retired)	1817.8	2795.5	5.38%

(MasterCard Asia/Pacific, Asian Demographics)

All lifecycle stages will be expanding in the Philippines in the next decade as shown in Chart 2.10. The elderly women population will be quite small as a percentage of the total. In 2004 it was 4%, and is expected to be 6% in 2014.

Chart 2.10
THE PHILIPPINES: Women by Numbers

(Asian Demographics)

WOMEN CONSUMERS IN ASIA

INDIA

India's population is also very young. Today the average age of all Indians is 28, and it will rise to only 33 by 2014. Population growth will stay relatively high at an annual rate of 2%.

All four women population segments are set to grow in the next decade. The empty nesters segment will be the fastest growing at a rate of 6% per year. The next highest is the elderly households segment at 4%, followed by the middle aged households with children segment at 2% and young households segment will grow the slowest at just below 2%. But this segment is huge. Its size in 2004 was 215 million and is expected to expand to 248 million in 10 years' time. In spite of its lower growth rates, it will still be almost double the combined population size of the other three segments. Young women therefore dominate the women population in India.

Table 2.13
INDIA: Women Population (Individuals)

INDIA (000)	2004	2014	Av. Annual Growth Rate
Young Households	215122.9	247986.5	1.53%
Middle Aged Households with Children	84887.5	102502.6	2.08%
Empty Nesters (working)	24613.8	39205.0	5.93%
Elderly Households (retired)	24496.8	34100.1	3.92%

(MasterCard Asia/Pacific, Asian Demographics)

All the lifecycle stages are set to expand in the coming decade. The young singles segment is expected to grow relatively fast as well, which is an interesting indicator of the beginning of an emerging trend of young people getting married later in India. As mentioned above, young women dominate in India. Accordingly, women over 65 years old accounted for only 5% of all women in 2004; and will account for 6% in 2014.

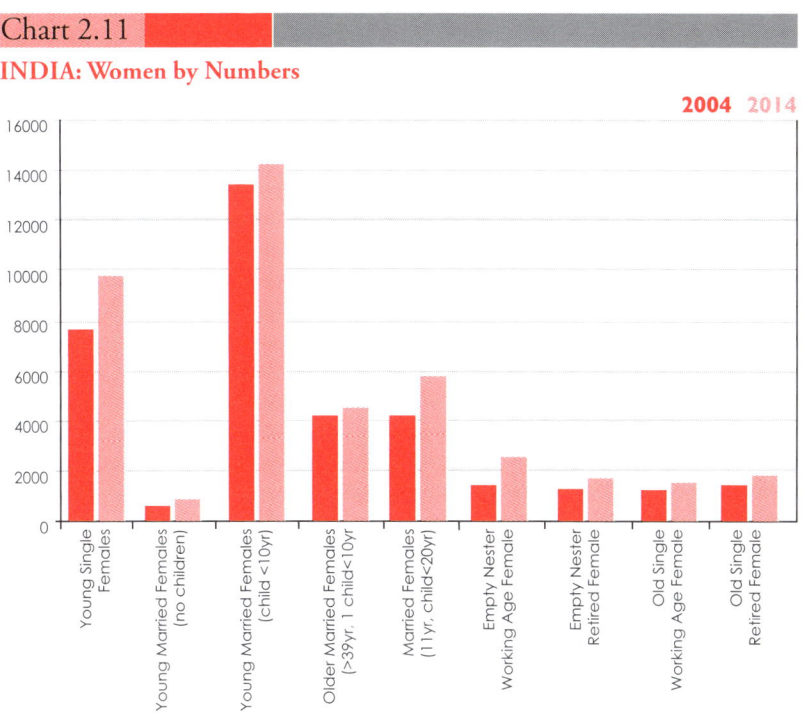

Chart 2.11

INDIA: Women by Numbers

(Asian Demographics)

SUMMARY

In spite of their very different stages of economic development and income levels, market sizes and rates of population growth, all these markets have in common the rising clout of their women consumers. In Japan, it is the elderly women that will hold sway in the coming years, whereas in India the young and well educated women in urban areas will lead. For businesses in the consumer markets of Asia, they are shaping new business opportunities and offering up enticing rewards to those who succeed.

WOMEN CONSUMERS IN AFFLUENT ASIA: JAPAN & KOREA 3

The women from the 11 countries covered in this book can be split into two groups. The first are the women of "affluent" Asia, i.e., those from countries with relatively developed economies. These are countries where the average annual income is over $13,000 a year and runs as high as $37,000 a year (Japan). The countries in this category are Australia, Hong Kong, Japan, Korea, Singapore and Taiwan.

The second group comprises women from poorer emerging countries such as China, India, Malaysia, the Philippines and Thailand, where the average income is below $13,000 a year.

Marked contrasts exist between these two groups (and there are also differences within each group). Those wishing to tap into these markets need to understand these nuances. The following chapters will cover the countries of affluent Asia first, with a separate chapter on Australia. Among emerging Asia, it will be in a similar format, with a chapter just on China, the biggest market of all.

JAPAN

SNAPSHOT

population: 128 million
per capita income: $37,000
economic growth: 2.6%
(2004)

Japan stands out in several regards. For one, it is the world's second largest economy despite a decade of recession. For another, it is arguably the world's first "super-ageing" society. Japan has been called a "dying" nation, since it has a declining fertility rate and an ageing population (making some of the biggest growth opportunities in areas such as health care and funeral parlors). Japan's fertility rate[1] declined to 1.29 children per woman in 2003—far below replacement level.

Chart 3.1
A RAPIDLY AGEING POPULATION: Japan - Age Profile 2005, 2020

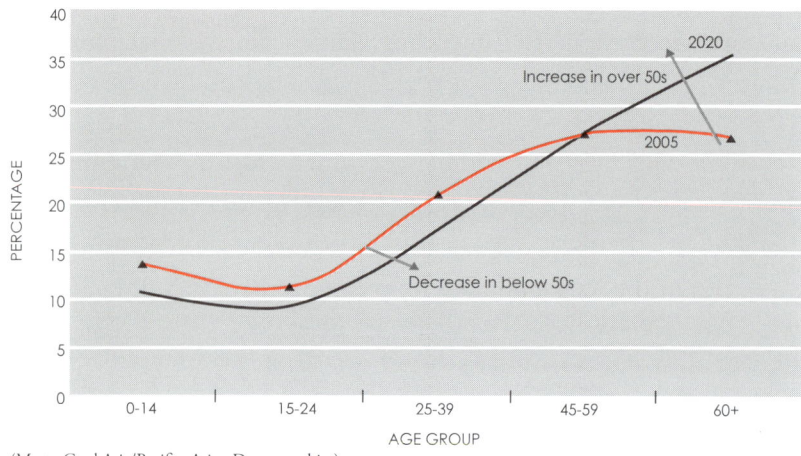

(MasterCard Asia/Pacific, Asian Demographics)

Currently, women outlive men by about a decade. It is expected that they will outlive men by even more in the future. As illustrated in Chart 3.2, the population is about evenly split between men and women. By age 70, the ratio rises to 1.3 women for every man. For those 75 and older, it rises to 1.7 women per man, a ratio of nearly two to one.

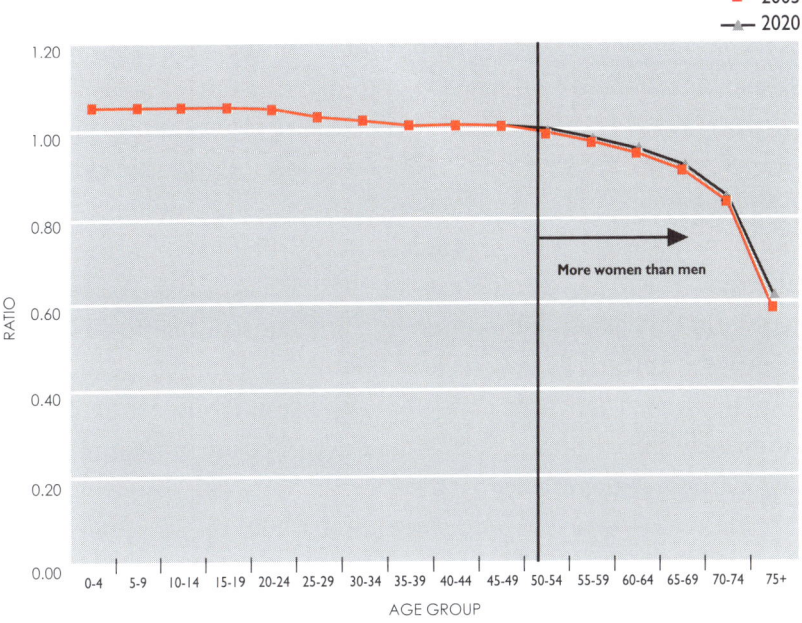

Chart 3.2
MORE ELDERLY WOMEN THAN MEN:
Japan Male to Female Ratio

(MasterCard Asia/Pacific, Asian Demographics)

What makes Japan a "super-ageing" society is that, while its demographic trends have much in common with some developed countries in the West, notably Italy and Sweden, it is unique in its steadfast refusal to open its doors to immigrants to compensate for its shrinking and ageing population. As a result, elderly women in Japan have an emerging and increasingly important role as consumers.

HOWL OF THE "LOSER DOGS"

One reason for Japan's declining fertility is that women are marrying later, or, increasingly, not marrying at all. For example, the number of unmarried Japanese women, ages 30 to 34, almost doubled from 14% to 27% between 1990 and 2000. Similarly, the number of unmarried women 35 to 39 increased from 8% to 14%. An astonishing 54% of women in their 20s are single. Japan has come a long way from when most women were expected to be married by the age of 25, and any woman older than that was dismissed as "old Christmas cake."

A popular term has been coined by the bestselling author Junko Sakai, *makeinu* (loser dogs), to describe single career women in their 30s. Her best-selling novel is called *Makeinu no Toobo* or "Howl of the Loser Dogs." Her book contrasted *makeinu* with *kachiinu* (winner dogs), who are married with children.[2] "Loser dogs" bemoan the lack of suitable men. They have cash to spare and they love to pamper themselves—visit beauty salons, health spas and follow the latest fashion trends. Time not spent raising children is devoted to careers, and to new hobbies, learning new languages and traditional Japanese crafts. Savings are used to decorate their homes lavishly. Princess Sayako had even become a role model as the top "loser dog," possible even in the imperial household. But her marriage—at age 36—to a commoner (and the stripping of her imperial title) may not be much inspiration for loser dogs.

There is an ongoing and lively debate on the desirability and socioeconomic consequences of "loser dogs" and "winner dogs" in Japan. From a demographic point of view, the consequences of the "loser dogs" trend is clear—several decades of low birth rates are flattening the age-curve of first time mothers. Japanese women are having babies both at a younger age (the "winner dogs") and at a later age (the "loser dogs" who finally find their men).

Chart 3.3
Flattening of the Age-Curve of Mothers
Live Births by Age of Mother

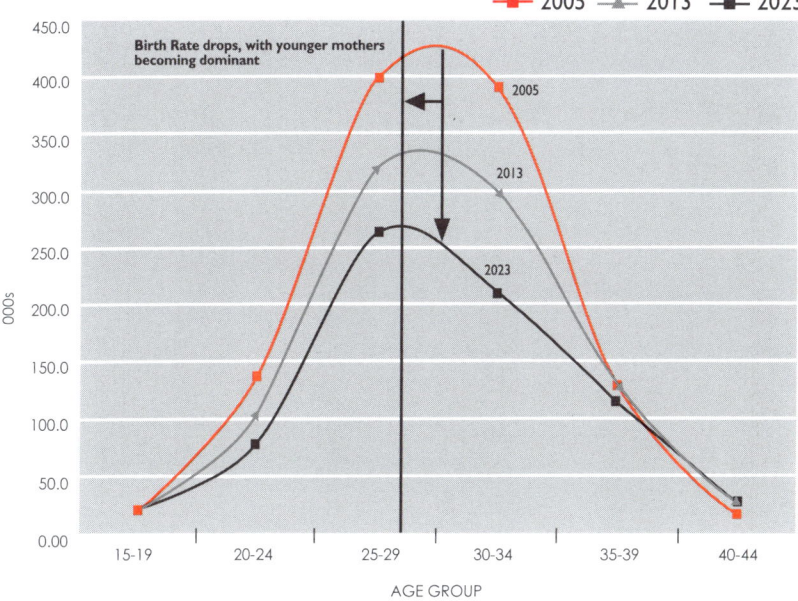

(MasterCard Asia/Pacific, Asian Demographics)

RISE OF THE EMPTY NESTERS

At the other end of the spectrum from the unmarried younger women, the "loser dogs," are the empty nesters. Since women outlive men by a wide margin, many of the empty nester households eventually turn into single-person households that comprise elderly women. In 2004, a third of the elderly (65+) were living only with their spouses, and one seventh of them were living alone. In the coming decade, the latter percentage is set to rise fast as more and more single elderly women will be living on their own. This trend is reflected in a simultaneous increase in the number of households and decrease in household size as illustrated by Chart 3.4.

Chart 3.4
Simultaneous Increase in Number of Households & Decrease in Household Size - Japan: Households & Household size

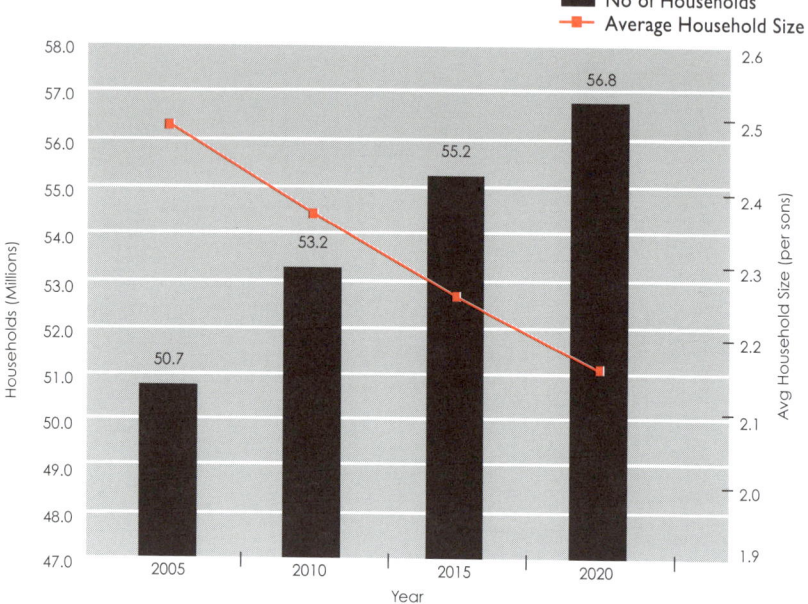

(MasterCard Asia/Pacific, Asian Demographics)

The emerging lifestyle and spending patterns of these elderly single women will dominate the shape and size of the women consumer market in Japan in the coming years.

WOMEN'S ROLE IN THE WORK FORCE

Twenty years after the enactment of the Equal Employment Opportunity Law (in 1985), women's participation in the labor force remains marginal. In 2003, only 3% of all company directors and 5% of managers were women in Japan's corporate sector. Most women are employed in part-time work, defined as working less than 34 hours a week. In 2004, there were over a million women part-time workers in Japan, accounting for about 90% of the total.

Women's marital status is a key determinant of their employment and income status. Typically, women leave the workforce after childbirth, and go back to work in their mid-40s when child rearing duties are reduced. This situation is reflected in the "M" curve pattern as shown in Chart 3.5.

Chart 3.5
Younger & Older Woman Dominate in the Labor Force Historically
The M Curve - Female Employees by Age Group (2004)

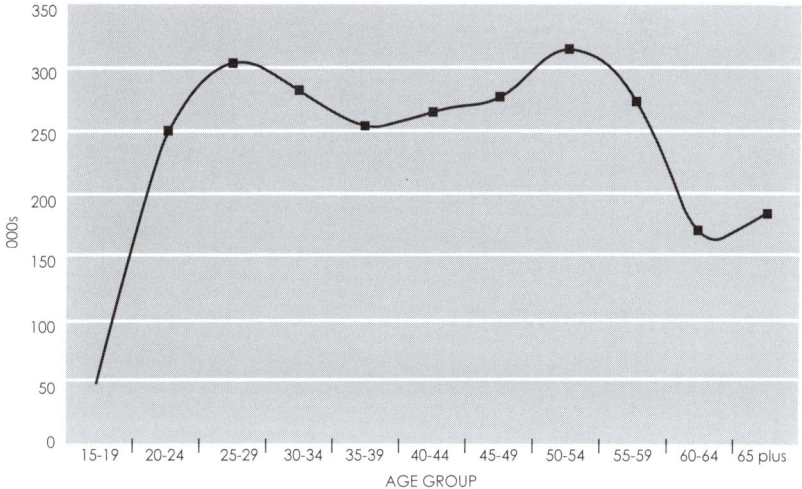

(MasterCard Asia/Pacific, Asian Demographics)

With the rise of the "loser dogs" phenomenon, the middle part of the "M" curve can be expected to flatten out, transforming it into more like an inverted "U" curve with a wide flat top in the coming decade. Prospects of improving employment and income status for Japanese women, however, are not encouraging. Japanese women are by and large well educated. But their education has yet to translate into better jobs and higher incomes. A stagnating economy is one reason. A second reason is that Japanese women tend to enroll in less rigorous, though expensive, junior colleges that do not require the same tough entrance examinations as for university admission. In the 1990s, for example, female students accounted for an average of only a quarter of the four-year university student population. This pattern is expected to remain intact in coming years.

With a slow growth economy, where new and good jobs are hard to come by, and a less competitive education background when compared with men, Japanese women's labor force participation is not expected to increase in the coming decades. The women's labor force participation rate, which has been hovering around 60% of those who are 15 to 64 years old, is likely to stay unchanged for the foreseeable future.

Women's consumption power in Japan, given the factors discussed above, would appear to be weak in comparison with men, and likely to stay weak in the future. This overall picture, however, hides an important segment that is poised to become more powerful and important in terms of their wealth, longevity and active lifestyles—Japan's elderly women.

THE EMERGING ROLE OF ELDERLY WOMEN

The older Japanese population continues to be economically active, often pushing back retirement age to 70 and above. Most of the so called "junior" seniors, those who are between 60 to 70 years old, are in good health and want to continue to work. Many are actually supporting their fully grown children. In a recent survey of those aged 60 to 64, 70% of men and 40% of women expressed their desire to continue working.[3]

Among the elderly, women will dominate. The emerging picture of the elderly in Japan, however, has become more complex. It is clear that they are healthier and lead more active lives than those a generation or two ago. It has been estimated that only 13% of those presently over 65 years old require regular care. There are a wide variety of organizations, many supported by the government, to serve as caregivers to the elderly. These include social welfare foundations, private companies and agricultural as well as consumer cooperatives. The government also launched the comprehensive Long-Term Care Insurance in 2000.

The Japanese elderly are not only relatively healthy, but they are also relatively prosperous. The average household income for an elderly person in Japan, irrespective of the type of household (empty nesters or old singles), is only 10% less than the overall household average. In addition to their relatively high income, the elderly also hold the largest share of accumulated privately held assets in Japan.[4] As much as 70% of all privately owned assets in the country, including all real estate assets, belong to those who are over 50 years old. Another indicator of the elderly people's financial strength is the amount of inheritance they leave behind. In the past 10 years, the average amount was $330,000, not an insignificant sum.

These healthy, active and financial well-endowed Japanese elderly have been characterized as the "silver aristocrats."[5] Their priorities in life are to:

- have time and space to do things by themselves;
- be free from excessive social demand;
- be able to pursue youthful lifestyles;
- be able to enjoy the finer things in life such as art and classical music, and
- be able to live for pure leisure.

As the Japanese are living longer and longer, it is possible actually to identify "sub-segments" among the elderly. There is a working population of elderly that is between 50 and 75 years old. After 75, the period of "old" old age begins. Indeed, there is a movement for seniors over 75 years old called "New Old People's Movement," founded by Dr. Hinohara Shigeaki, 92, a practicing medical doctor. He counsels the elderly that "the most important factor is one's outlook on life. Be optimistic. Enjoy new experiences. Do what you want to do."

Thus, these silver aristocrats are rather self-indulgent people, which resonates with Japan's traditional cultural values. Ruth Benedict, in her seminal study of prewar Japanese society,[6] made the profound observation that "the arc of life [in Japan] is plotted in opposite fashion to the United States. It is a great shallow U-curve, and maximum freedom and indulgence allowed to babies and the old." There is a traditional Japanese saying that the very old and very young must be indulged as they are "closer to God" (having just been born or approaching death) than the rest of the population.

Japan's highly urbanized society is also very conducive to the lifestyles of these silver aristocrats with a wide variety of leisure activities, entertainment and sophisticated amenities on tap. Indeed, the largest urban centers of Tokyo, Osaka and Nagoya have seen the fastest growth of the elderly in recent years. Again, this is a trend opposite to that of Western societies where the elderly tend to retire to the countryside. This trend makes the consumer market of the elderly easy for businesses to access.

These silver aristocrats will certainly continue to indulge themselves. They have increased their spending on education (a strong indicator of their lifestyle in seeking new challenges and pursuing new interests), recreation (including overseas travel), as well as on transportation and communications. The elderly between 60 and 75 spend most on socializing—spending time with friends and pursuing new hobbies together. The special needs of these silver aristocrats have given a boost to the service sector such as 24-hour convenience stores, department stores that feature more refined products, take away restaurants, health spas, continuing education centers, and amateur associations dedicated to the pursuit of a wide variety of hobbies and interests.

As mentioned above, when the empty nester households become the old singles households, it is the elderly women that are left in charge. Given that the average Japanese wife outlives her husband, to a large extent the silver aristocrat phenomenon is really about elderly women—in their 70s and above, living in urban areas, financially well-endowed, healthy and active, well networked and plugged into a sophisticated support system that caters to their needs and lifestyle pursuits.

THE EMERGING WOMEN CONSUMER OF JAPAN

The emerging women consumer market in Japan features two dominant lifecycle stages—the young singles and the old singles. The rise of the young singles is a consequence of the late marriage or no marriage trend. The rise of the old singles is a consequence of women's longevity and increasingly active lifestyles.

The total spending power of Japan's women consumers is estimated by the four key household segments. The young households are estimated to have collectively commanded some $515 billion of spending power in 2004, the largest among the four segments, but it will grow to only $530 billion[7] in 10 years' time. The middle aged household segment, with spending power of $234 billion in 2004, and the empty nesters segment, with spending power of $413 billion in 2004, will both see spending power grow only about 1% a year in the coming decade. In contrast, the elderly household segment, with a 2004 spending power of $360 billion, is expected to see the fastest growth, at an impressive annual rate of 5%.

From the point of view of spending per woman, however, the picture looks quite different. Women in the middle aged with children segment had the highest spending power at $24,800 in 2004, projected to rise to $32,447 in 2014. Women in the empty nesters segment have the second highest spending power per person. In 2004 their average spending was $29,300 per woman. By 2014, however, they will rise to become the top spenders at $33,470 per woman. Women in the elderly households segment rank third in per person spending in 2004 at $25,600 per woman, followed by women in the young household segment at $24,800 per woman.

Table 3.1

JAPAN: Women Consumers: Potential Spending Power by Household

US$Billions ($2004)	2004	2014	Av. Annual Growth Rate
Young Households	$514.7	$529.9	0.30%
Middle Aged Households with Children	$234.4	$261.3	1.15%
Empty Nesters (working)	$413.4	$455.5	1.02%
Elderly Households(retired)	$360.5	$525.9	4.59%

(MasterCard Asia/Pacific, Asian Demographics)

For elderly women, the demand for services is expected to be greater than demand for consumer goods and products. This is good news for businesses that are targeting this segment. Demand for consumer goods and products tends to have a low saturation threshold, whereas demand for services could expand virtually indefinitely as long as consumers are provided with new and satisfying experiences. The growth of demand for services is only limited by businesses' ability to innovate. The discretionary spending power of the four household segments is summarized in Table 3.2.

Table 3.2
JAPAN: Women Consumers: Total Discretionary Expenditures by Household

US$Billions ($2004)	2004	2014	Av. Annual Growth Rate
Young Households	$68.5	$68.1	-0.06%
Middle Aged Households with Children	$31.2	$33.6	0.76%
Empty Nesters (working)	$55.0	$58.6	0.64%
Elderly Households (retired)	$48.0	$67.6	4.09%

(MasterCard Asia/Pacific, Asian Demographics)

When discretionary spending is calculated on a per woman basis, however, women in the middle aged households become the top spenders. Their discretionary spending was $4,028 per woman in 2004, compared with $3,900 per woman in the empty nesters segment, $3,410 per woman in the elderly households segment, and $3,300 per woman in the young households segment. By 2014, women in the empty nesters segment are expected to become the top spenders, with discretionary spending power of over $4,000 per woman. They will be followed by women in the middle aged segment with $3,900 per woman; the elderly households segment with $3,400 per woman, and the young households segment with $3,300 per woman. Thus, on a per woman basis the young women of Japan have the lowest spending power, whereas older women in the empty nesters segment have the highest.

Discretionary spending can be further broken down into six key types of spending:

1) food and beverage: dining and special treats
2) personal care: cosmetics, beauty salon and related treatments

3) recreation and entertainment: travel, playing golf, going to concerts
4) household purchases: non-essential items to decorate the home
5) healthcare
6) transportation and communications

Japanese women spend most on recreation and entertainment and on food and beverage. But it is in recreation and entertainment that growth is expected to be highest in the coming decade.

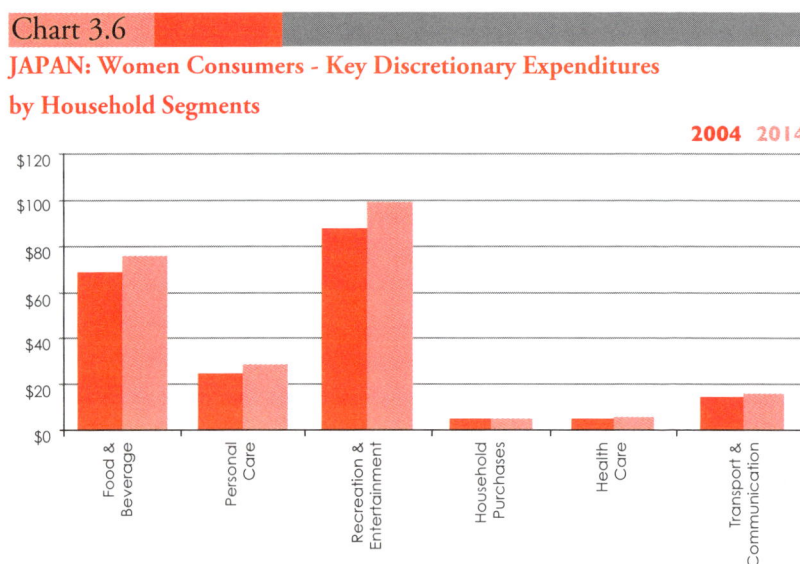

Chart 3.6
JAPAN: Women Consumers - Key Discretionary Expenditures by Household Segments

(MasterCard Asia/Pacific, Asian Demographics)

However one looks at it, Japanese women consumers are heavy hitters in terms of their purchasing power. With the exception of the young householders, per capita spending is expected to grow in all age segments, with the elderly householders leading. As mentioned, business opportunities in catering to Japanese women consumers will see rapid and exciting expansion in the coming decade. How well businesses can drive innovations to meet women's changing needs due to demographic and lifestyle changes will be the key to success.

KOREA

SNAPSHOT

population: 48 million
per capita income: $14,380
economic growth: 4.7%
(2004)

The growth of the Korean population has been slowing for some time. Between now and 2013, the average annual rate of population growth is expected to be only around 0.4%, down from the 1% annual growth rate of the past decade. While population growth is slowing, the ratio of females to males will rise.

Chart 3.7
Slowing Population Growth: Population Male to Female Ratio

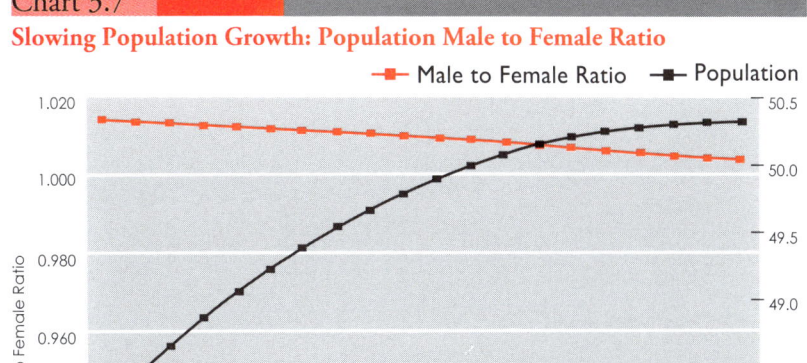

(MasterCard Asia/Pacific, Asian Demographics)

Among the population over 55 years of age, there will be more women than men. Indeed, by 2010, among those who are 75 years and older, it is expected that there will be five women for every man.

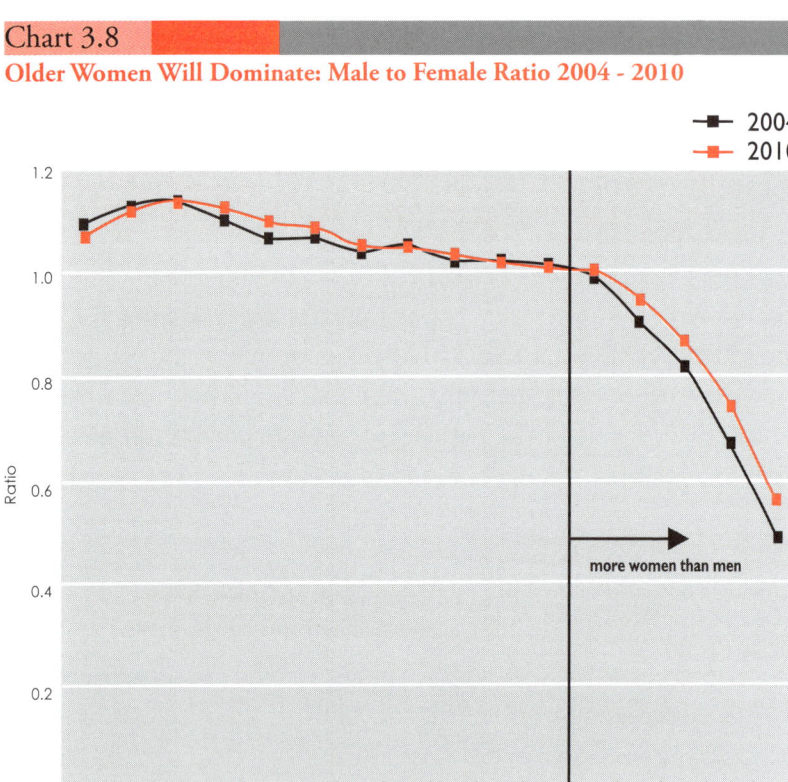

Chart 3.8
Older Women Will Dominate: Male to Female Ratio 2004 - 2010

(MasterCard Asia/Pacific, Asian Demographics)

Within the female population itself, the ageing trend is very clear. Between now and 2010, there will be a steady decline in women under 35 years old, and a corresponding increase in women over 40.

Chart 3.9

Changing Age Distribution of Women: Female Age Profile

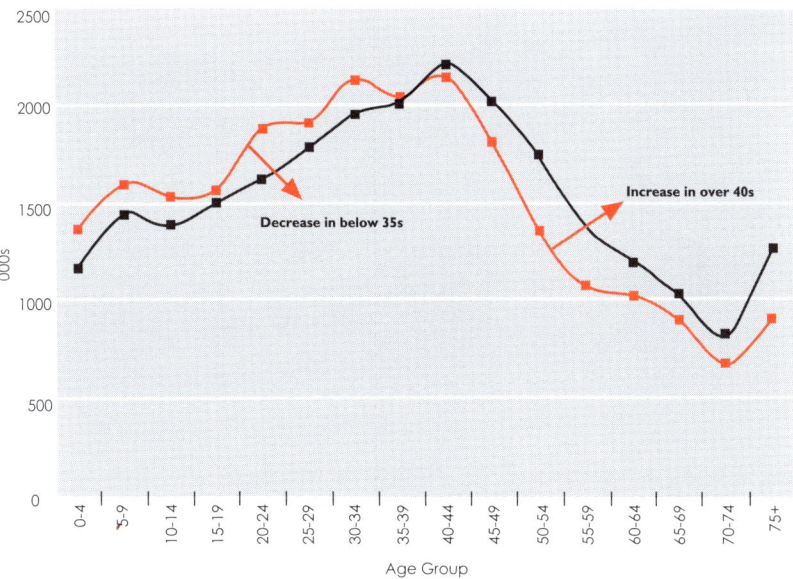

(MasterCard Asia/Pacific, Asian Demographics)

This trend has to do with Korea's dramatic declining birth rate, which has been dropping at an even faster rate than Japan's. In 2003, for example, Japan's birth rate was 1.3,[8] compared to 1.2 in South Korea, a big drop from the 4.6 children in 1970. While most Korean women are still choosing to marry, a large number are deciding either not to have children or to postpone having them. The high cost of raising children, of which the costs of education are expected to be the most burdensome, is frequently cited as a reason. Underpinning this phenomenon is, of course, a sea change in lifestyles and family structures.

Even among couples who opt to have children, they tend to compress their reproductive lives into a relatively short span. They typically have children soon after marriage and the woman would likely quit her job to stay home. But the norm is to have a single child, which allows women to be free from their child-rearing activities by their early 30s.

WOMEN'S CHANGING ROLES

Korean women have made great strides in education in the past few decades. In the 1970s, few women went to college. Today more than a quarter do so. In terms of the four-year university program, women account for about 38% of total enrolment. The women-only universities in Korea are especially influential, and they are at the forefront of the latest technology. Ewha Women's University, for example, now offers online courses to some 30 universities around the world.

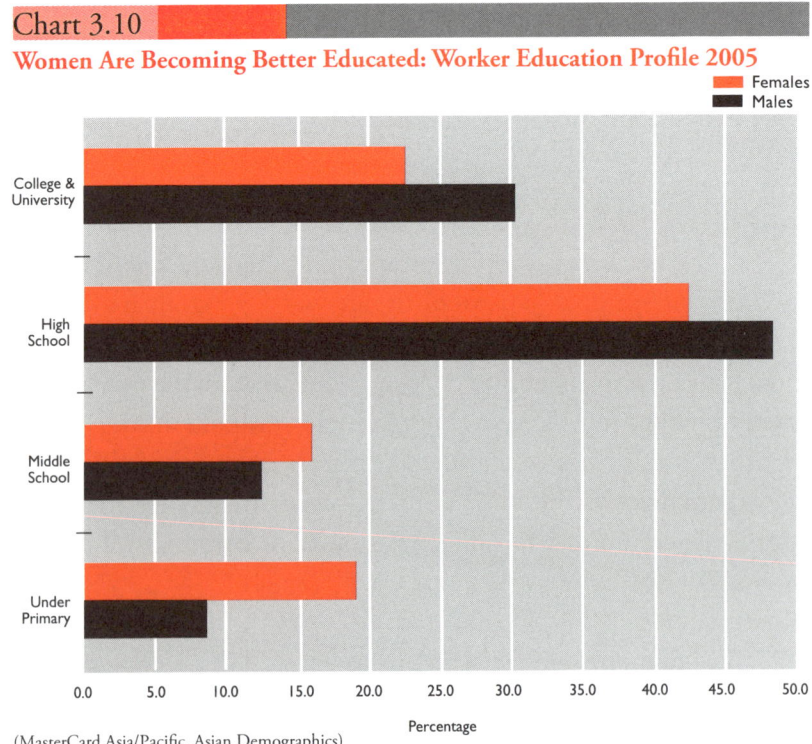

Chart 3.10
Women Are Becoming Better Educated: Worker Education Profile 2005

(MasterCard Asia/Pacific, Asian Demographics)

While the traditional Confucian value system is still prevalent in Korea, the role of women has been changing fast. Women today have full equal legal rights, and a Ministry of Gender Equality was established in 2001. Despite all this progress, Korean women are still under-represented in the work force. Today, women account for 41% of the work force, and it is still very rare to find women in senior management positions.

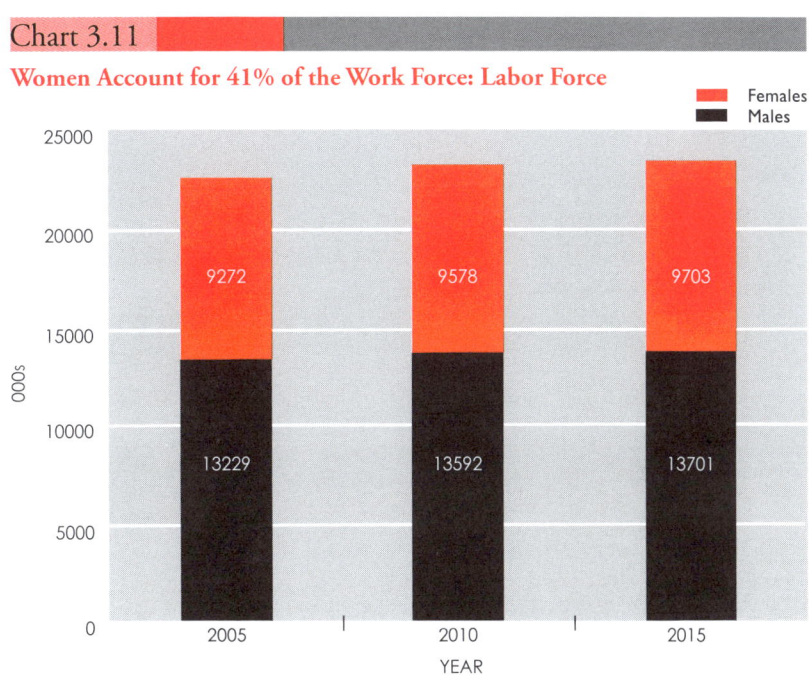

Chart 3.11
Women Account for 41% of the Work Force: Labor Force

(MasterCard Asia/Pacific, Asian Demographics)

Among women who are in the work force, most are in the informal and "subcontracting" sectors (the latter is defined as firms employing fewer than five workers). A recent trend is for younger women to migrate from manufacturing to services—both because of the shrinking of manufacturing employment and because of better working conditions in the service sector.

A more important trend, however, is that women tend to be self-employed and running small businesses. While women are in charge of about 36% of all businesses, women-run businesses tend to employ women—71% of women's employees are women, doubling the national average.[9] Women businesses are also concentrated in certain sectors. Women own 68% of food and lodging businesses and 57% of education service businesses. In contrast, they run only 16% of manufacturing businesses.

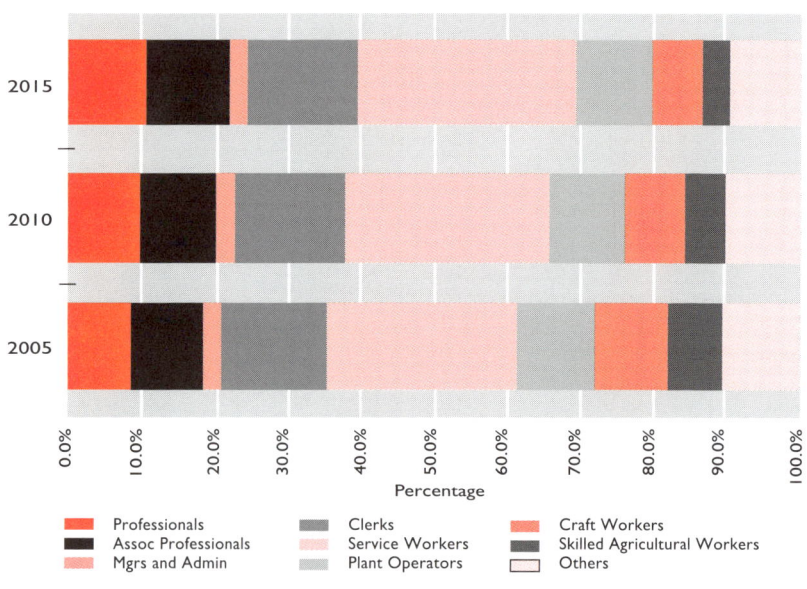

Chart 3.12
Rising Importance of the Service Sector: Employment by Category

Professionals | Clerks | Craft Workers
Assoc Professionals | Service Workers | Skilled Agricultural Workers
Mgrs and Admin | Plant Operators | Others

(MasterCard Asia/Pacific, Asian Demographics)

Overall, women's businesses have been assessed as well run. The average debt of women's enterprises is around 64% of annual turnover, compared with the national average of 174%. These businesses are, however, behind in the use of information and communications technologies. It is estimated that only 34% of them use computers, and only 4% have websites, with fewer than

1% doing online transactions. This condition is largely due to their small size and the sectors in which they operate.

But manufacturing, the traditional powerhouse, is shrinking. Services are set to become more important in the future, which will place women-run businesses in the driver's seat in terms of employment and income generation.

Finance, real estate, wholesale and retail are expected to become the dominant employment sectors in the next decade. With women's improving education profile, the rising role of the service sectors will help to further improve Korean women's socioeconomic status in the coming years.

Chart 3.13
Finance, Real Estate and the Trades Are Key Employment Sectors: Employment by Industry

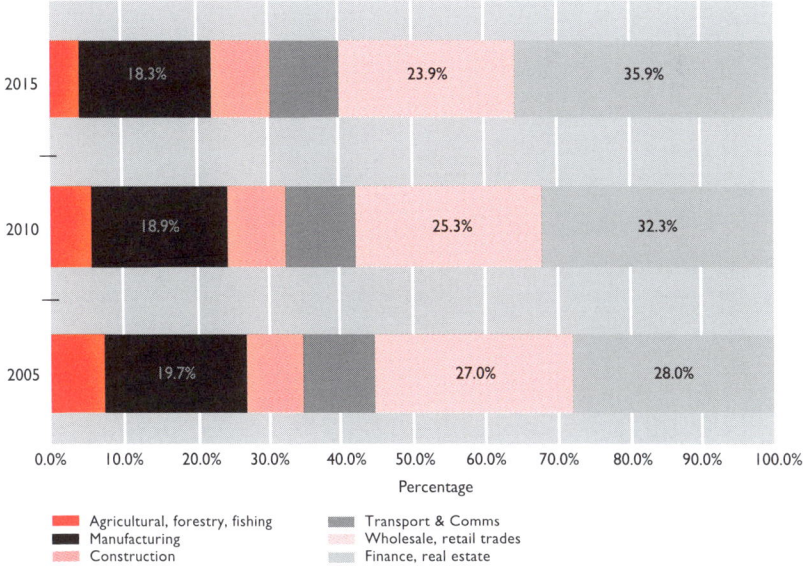

(MasterCard Asia/Pacific, Asian Demographics)

HOUSEHOLD FORMATION AND CONSUMPTION DYNAMICS

South Korea is a highly urbanized society, with more than three quarters of the population living in urban areas. The declining population growth rates would mean smaller household size, but as more young people opt for a single and independent lifestyle, many of them will also set up their own households outside of the traditional extended family context. This trend leads to smaller but more numerous households, an atomization of the traditional household.

Chart 3.14
Declining Household Size but More Households:
Households & Average Household Size

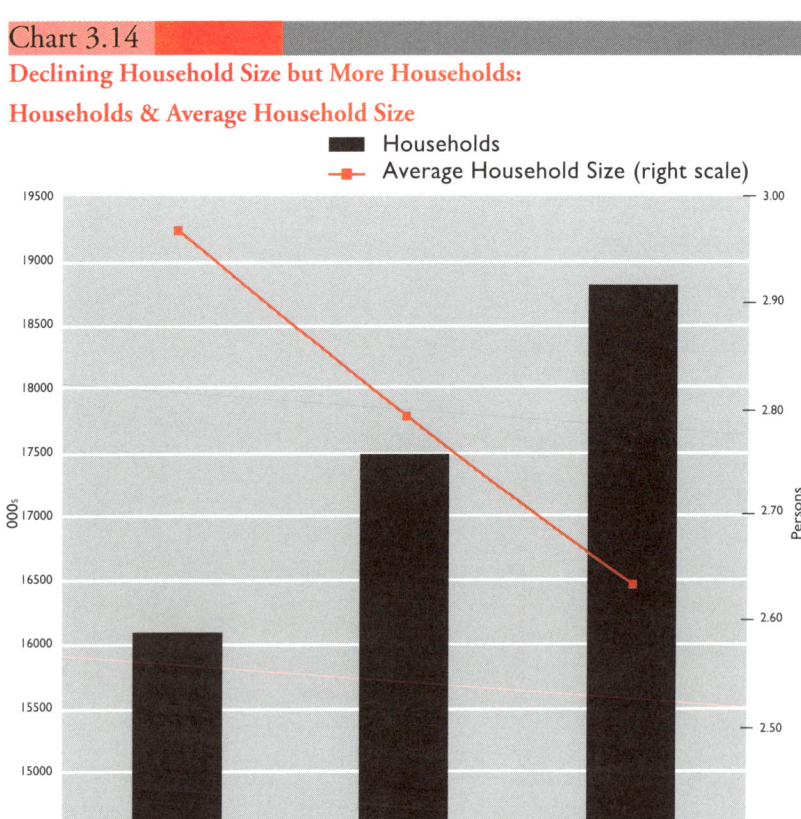

(MasterCard Asia/Pacific, Asian Demographics)

At a projected growth rate of 5% a year, and with the rising number of households, growth per household is expected to be about 2% per year over the coming decade. From a lifecycle stage point of view, this means that young singles households will dominate, followed by young married households What results is a unique composite of generations in Korea in the next decade, and this sets the stage for major cultural changes to take place, especially those involving women.

In modern Korean history, three generations occupy the driver's seat in terms of ushering in changes. The first were the baby boomers, who were born after the 1950-53 Korean War. Women baby boomers, now in their 50s, have been the beneficiaries of a great deal of social change and new freedom. They are the in-between generation of those who were brought up with conservative traditional values, but who are also progressive, embracing educational opportunities, family planning and career development.

The second are the "386 generation," referring to those who are in their 30s and 40s, educated in the '80s, and were born in the '60s. This is a pivotal generation. They are affluent, well-educated and liberal. Now entering their 40s, they are the driving force of change in Korean society. Women in this generation are the pioneers in defining their new-earned status and economic positions in the society.

The third are the "N-generation" (the Net generation), who are in their 20s. They were born after the tech revolution in the late 1970s and 1980s, and are at home in cyberspace. They embody South Korea's advanced development in information technology. They grew up during South Korea's economic boom, and had more money to spend on leisure than their parents and grandparents. Women of this generation are shaping South Korea's demographic and lifestyle trends, which will have a far-reaching impact in the coming decade.

These generational perspectives, in consumer marketing terms, mean rising importance of three key consumer segments: the young women households, working empty nesters women households, and old single women households. By 2013, for example, empty nesters and old singles are expected to account for over 36% of women, while young singles will account for about 35% of women in Korea.

In 2004, these three women consumer segments' total spending power was estimated at $209 billion, of which the young households segment accounted for the lion's share with $106 billion, over 50%. By 2014, their collective spending power is expected to reach $307 billion, with the empty nesters segment growing at the fastest rate of 9%. The young households segment will still be the biggest spenders, accounting for 43% of the total. The elderly household segment's spending power is quite small in comparison, estimated at $24 billion in 2004. But this segment will see its spending power grow at the highest annual rate of 13% to reach $56 billion in 10 years' time.

From the perspective of spending power per person, the picture looks very different. Women in the middle aged households segment have the highest spending power per woman. Average spending per woman was about $14,600 in 2004. Women in the empty nesters segment have the second highest spending, at $13,200 per woman. Women in the young households segment come third, at $11,100 per woman. Women in the elderly households segment come last, at $10,000 per woman. By 2014, women in the elderly households segment will have caught up with the young households segment, taking third place. So on a per woman basis, women in the young households segment will have the lowest spending power in 10 years' time.

Table 3.3
KOREA: Women Consumers: Potential Spending Power by Household

US$Billions ($2004)	2004	2014	Av. Annual Growth Rate
Young Households	$106.0	$131.5	2.41%
Middle Aged Households with Children	$47.2	$73.6	5.59%
Empty Nesters (working)	$55.1	$102.2	8.56%
Elderly Households (retired)	$24.4	$55.6	12.81%

(MasterCard Asia/Pacific, Asian Demographics)

The discretionary spending estimates of the four household segments are summarized in Table 3.4. Similar to the pattern of total spending, the elderly households' segment will be growing the fastest at an annual rate of 11%, followed by the empty nesters at 7%, middle aged households at 4% and young households at 1%.

Table 3.4
KOREA: Women Consumers: Total Discretionary Expenditures by Household

US$Billions ($2004)	2004	2014	Av. Annual Growth Rate
Young Households	$13.8	$15.8	1.39%
Middle Aged Households with Children	$6.2	$8.8	4.31%
Empty Nesters (working)	$7.2	$12.2	7.03%
Elderly Households (retired)	$3.2	$6.7	10.94%

(MasterCard Asia/Pacific, Asian Demographics)

At $14 billion, women in the young households segment have the highest total discretionary spending. From the perspective of discretionary spending per woman, it is women in the middle aged households segment that have the highest spending power, at

$1,900 in 2004. This is followed by the empty nesters, at $1,733 per woman, and the young households segment, at $1,450 per woman. Women in the elderly households segment have the lowest per woman spending, at $1,300. In 2014, this ranking will remain roughly the same.

The discretionary spending patterns of Korean women are illustrated in Chart 3.15. Dining out, buying wine, beer and spirits, and delicacies are the biggest item of expenditure, and also the second fastest growing one. Recreation and entertainment are the second biggest, but the fastest growing. This is followed by personal care, transportation and communication, household purchases and health care. By 2014, it is expected that total discretionary spending by Korean women will reach $363 billion.

Chart 3.15
KOREA: Women Consumers - Key Discretionary Expenditures by Household Segments

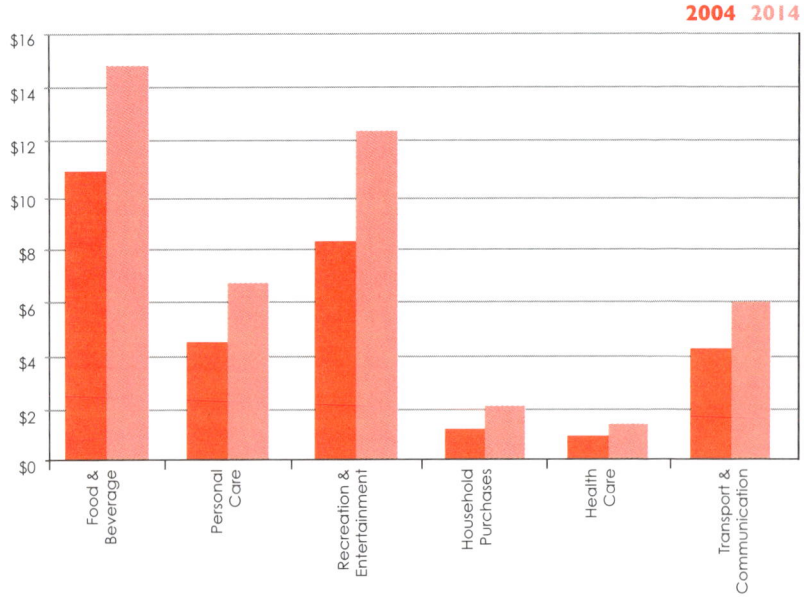

(MasterCard Asia/Pacific, Asian Demographics)

Remarkable changes are underway in both Japan and Korea among the women population. The women in both countries today and more so in the future will have the well-being, resources and social freedom to become an even more powerful consumer force than they are today. These women will in large measure help determine the size, shape and evolution of their respective economies in the years ahead. In the next chapter we will look at the rest of affluent Asia and the revolution underway for their female inhabitants.

WOMEN CONSUMERS IN AFFLUENT ASIA: TAIWAN, HONG KONG & SINGAPORE

4

After Japan and Korea, the three markets of Taiwan, Hong Kong and Singapore are also considered part of affluent Asia—all are highly developed economies with per capita GDP over $13,000.

TAIWAN

SNAPSHOT

population: 23 million
per capita income: $14,000
economic growth: 5.7%
(2004)

Taiwan's population is forecast to grow at only 0.5% a year from now to 2014 when it will be just under 24 million. The population is ageing, with those over 45 increasing and those under 30 declining As is true across Asia, women will outlive men. In the coming decade, there will be an increase of some 1.3 million women over the age of 50, compared with an increase of only 0.9 million men over the age of 50.

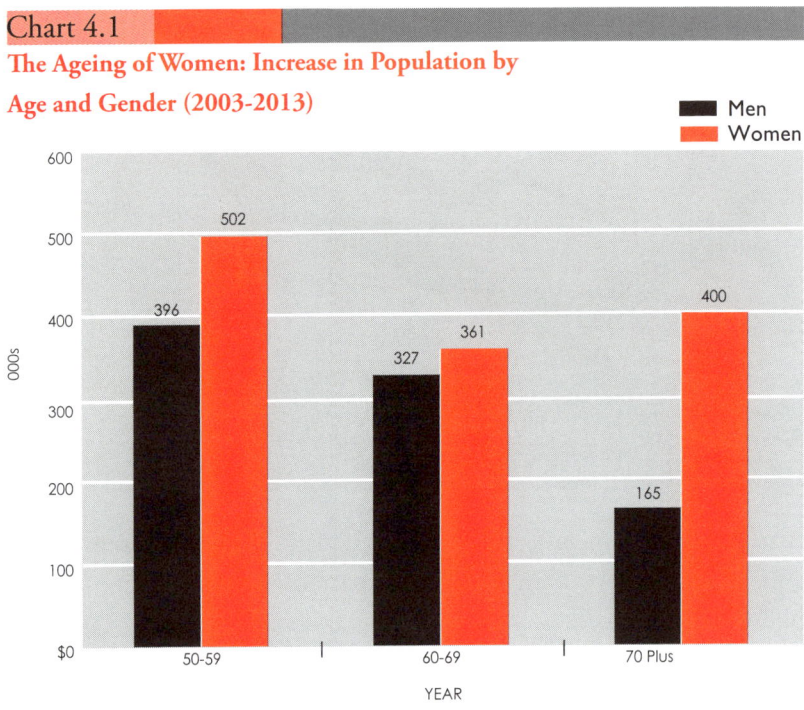

Chart 4.1
The Ageing of Women: Increase in Population by Age and Gender (2003-2013)

(MasterCard Asia/Pacific, Asian Demographics)

Apart from the ageing population (and the ageing of women), another major trend is urbanization. Both rural and town populations will decline in the coming decade, while the number of those living in cities will increase. By 2014, over two thirds of the total population will be living in cities. Together, cities and towns will account for almost 95% of the population, making Taiwan a fully urbanized society. This trend is an important variable in shaping Taiwan's future consumer market.

Chart 4.2

Urbanization Will Continue: Population by Segments

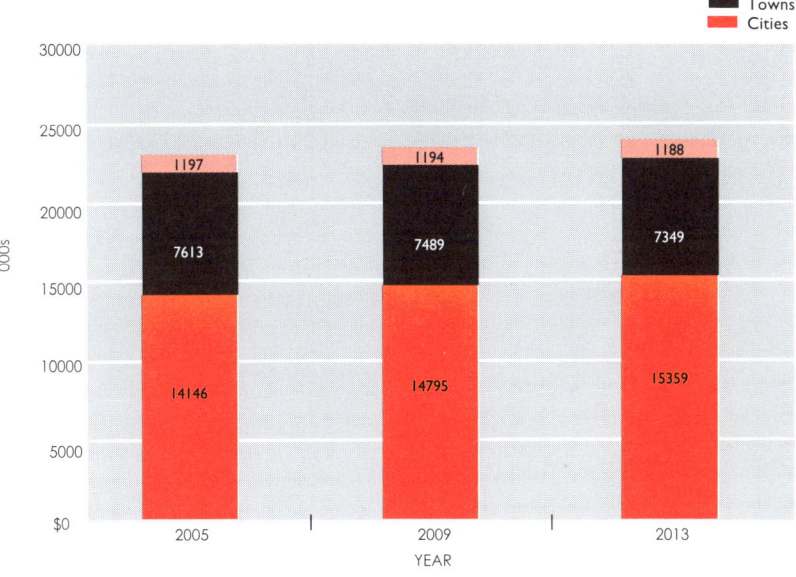

(MasterCard Asia/Pacific, Asian Demographics)

Average household size, however, will decline. The average city household, now about three persons, will decline to about 2.8 persons by 2014. Most households are having fewer children, while many will have no children at all. Overall fertility is on the decline, consistent with the declining population. Births per thousand women have dropped from 43 in 1996 to 41 today, and will drop even more, to 40 by 2014. Some 41% of households were without any dependent children in 2004 (empty nesters), and this figure is expected to rise to 55% by 2014.

RISING ROLE OF WOMEN IN THE ECONOMY

A major development is the rising economic clout of women. As men die out faster than women and fewer children are being born to join the workforce, women will have to take up the slack. The male labor force will decline by 0.03% a year while the female labor force will grow by 0.3% a year to 2014. In 1978, just over a tenth of small and medium enterprises (SMEs) were owned by women. By 2003, they owned around 16% of SMEs. Women entrepreneurs' role is expanding because more are better educated, they benefit from the expansion of the service sector, and they get government support such as SME loans programs. Today, a third of all business enterprises are headed by women in Taiwan.

The importance of women in the labor force is accentuated by the fact that many of Taiwan's best-educated men are working in China. Estimates differ, but a safe guess is about one million Taiwanese, nearly all of them men, are working on the mainland, managing the huge Taiwanese investments there. Given the growth of China's economy, it is likely that even more Taiwanese men will need to go to the mainland to oversee factories there. Thus women are set to become the real backbone of Taiwan's labor force.

Women consumers' spending power in the four consumer groups is illustrated in Table 4.1. The growth of young households spending power is the lowest, at about 0.7% a year to reach $44 billion by 2014. The growth of spending power of middle aged households with children is higher, at an average of 3% a year. In 2014, their spending power is projected to be $25 billion. The working empty nesters households will see their total spending power rising even faster, at 4%. In 2014, they will have $30 billion in spending power. The elderly retired households, however, are set to grow the fastest at 7% a year, with their total spending power reaching $18 billion in 2014.

Middle aged households have the largest spending power at $12,900 per woman. They are followed by the empty nesters at

$11,000. Next are elderly households at $10,500. Women in young households actually come last at $9,400. This ranking will hold for the next 10 years, with spending by empty nesters growing the fastest at 1.3% a year.

Table 4.1
TAIWAN: Women Consumers: Potential Spending Power by Household

US$Billions ($2004)	2004	2014	Av. Annual Growth Rate
Young Households	$42.7	$44.3	0.37%
Middle Aged Households with Children	$20.0	$25.2	2.60%
Empty Nesters (working)	$21.0	$29.7	4.14%
Elderly Households (retired)	$10.9	$18.3	6.77%

(MasterCard Asia/Pacific, Asian Demographics)

In discretionary spending, the pattern is similar but the growth for all four groups is higher than the growth in total spending. Discretionary spending by young households will reach $9 billion in 2014. For middle aged households, it will be $5 billion, and $6 billion for the working empty nesters households, and $4 billion for the elderly retired households. Again, women in middle aged households have the highest discretionary spending, at $2,500 per woman. Women in young households have the lowest, at $1,800. Women in empty nesters and elderly households rank second and third, with $2,160 and $2,055, respectively.

Table 4.2
TAIWAN: Women Consumers: Total Discretionary Expenditures by Household

US$Billions ($2004)	2004	2014	Av. Annual Growth Rate
Young Households	$8.4	$8.8	0.55%
Middle Aged Households with Children	$3.9	$5.0	2.82%
Empty Nesters (working)	$4.1	$5.9	4.39%
Elderly Households (retired)	$2.1	$3.6	7.06%

(MasterCard Asia/Pacific, Asian Demographics)

Spending on recreation and entertainment is now the largest item, and is projected to be the fastest growing. In 2014, women will be spending close to $14 billion on personal travel, and on recreational activities such as going to the theater, attending cultural and artistic events, visiting spas, hot springs and health resorts, and other leisure-related pursuits.

Chart 4.3
TAIWAN: Women Consumers: Key Discretionary Expenditures by Household Segments

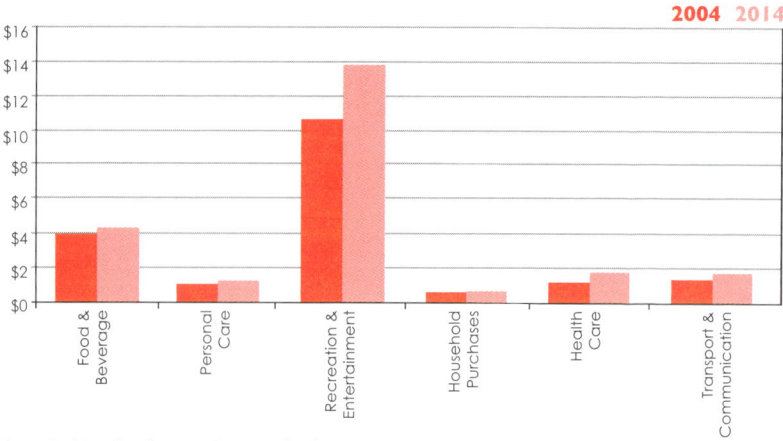

(MasterCard Asia/Pacific, Asian Demographics)

Taiwanese women's high spending on entertainment and recreation, both in absolute terms and in growth rates, means ample opportunities for businesses to grow in these areas as well as for new and innovative services to develop, especially those consistent with Taiwan's increasingly pervasive urban lifestyles.

HONG KONG

> **SNAPSHOT**
>
> population: 7 million
> per capita income: $24,000
> economic growth: 8.1%
> (2004)

Hong Kong's population is the second oldest in Asia after Japan. Among women, over the next decade, young households will shrink 1% a year while the older groups of empty nesters and elderly households are set to grow strongly, by 6% and 4% a year, respectively. Some 1.6 million women will be in empty nesters and elderly households versus 1.2 million in young households. This rapidly ageing trend is taking place during a major structural transformation of the economy. In the past two decades, Hong Kong has moved from being a manufacturing base to a provider of services, mostly due to the mainland being a much cheaper place for manufacturing.

The service sector accounted for about two-thirds of the economy in the 1980s. Today it is roughly 90%. The transformation of the job market has been even more dramatic. The wholesale and retail, import/export, restaurants and hotel services today employ about one fourth of all workers. High-end professional services such as finance, real estate and business services employ another 15%. Manufacturing, on the other hand, accounts for a puny 7% of the labor force.

Underpinning this transformation is the emergence of investment finance overtaking trade finance as a core activity of Hong Kong financiers. Hong Kong is benefiting from its unique position as a financial hub supporting China-centered investment finance, which turns out to be an even more powerful engine of job creation for high-end professional services than trade finance.

Educated women, both young and old, benefit from this trend. Better jobs for women translate directly into higher spending power. For women in young households, their total spending power should grow only marginally at 0.6% a year to $19 billion by 2014, since their numbers will actually shrink. For middle aged households with children, their total spending power will grow 3% a year in the next decade also to reach $19 billion by 2014. The working empty nesters will have the highest growth in total spending power at an impressive 11% a year. By 2014, they will command $22 billion in spending power. The elderly retired households will also see their total spending power grow, by 8% a year. Their total spending is expected to reach $1 billion by 2014.

In spending per woman, however, the situation is quite different. Women in middle aged households have the highest spending power, at $22,500 per woman, a much higher figure than the $18,500, $15,000 and $13,300 per woman respectively, for the empty nesters, elderly households and young households groups.

Table 4.3
HONG KONG: Women Consumers: Potential Spending Power by Household

US$Billions ($2004)	2004	2014	Av. Annual Growth Rate
Young Households	$18.2	$19.3	0.59%
Middle Aged Households with Children	$14.5	$19.4	3.30%
Empty Nesters (working)	$10.9	$21.9	10.7%
Elderly Households (retired)	$6.6	$12.0	8.24%

(MasterCard Asia/Pacific, Asian Demographics)

Their spending power can be divided into discretionary and nondiscretionary spending as shown in Table 4.3. The growth of the four groups' discretionary spending is similar to the growth of their total spending. By 2014, their discretionary spending is expected to reach $2.3 billion, $2.4 billion, $2.7 billion and $1.5 billion, respectively for the young households, the middle aged households with children, the working empty nesters and the retired elderly households.

Again, on a per woman basis, middle aged households have the highest discretionary spending power, at $2,700 per woman, followed by empty nesters, at $2,330 per woman, and elderly households, at $1,800 per woman. Those in young households have the lowest discretionary spending at $1,600 per woman.

Table 4.4
HONG KONG: Women Consumers: Total Discretionary Expenditures by Household

US$Billions ($2004)	2004	2014	Av. Annual Growth Rate
Young Households	$8.4	$2.3	0.68%
Middle Aged Households with Children	$1.8	$2.4	3.41%
Empty Nesters (working)	$1.3	$2.7	10.24%
Elderly Households (retired)	$0.8	$1.5	8.39%

(MasterCard Asia/Pacific, Asian Demographics)

Unlike their Taiwanese counterparts, Hong Kong women's discretionary spending is focused on food and beverage. This expenditure not only dwarfs all other discretionary items, but it is also expected to be the fastest growing. Expenditures on personal care, recreation and entertainment, household purchases, and transportation and communication trail far behind, with health care being the lowest.

Chart 4.4
HONG KONG: Women Consumers: Key Discretionary Expenditures by Household Segments

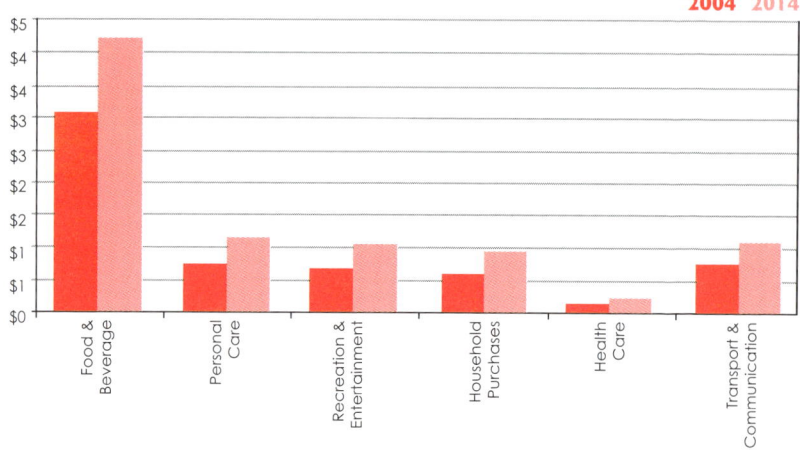

(MasterCard Asia/Pacific, Asian Demographics)

In Hong Kong's urban lifestyles, business competition in the food and beverage sector is intense, and it is set to become even more so in the future. Service innovations in creating new and exciting experiences in dining out and entertaining will be the new business driver; supplementing the traditional criterion of high quality cuisine, for example.

SINGAPORE

SNAPSHOT

population:	3 million
per capita income:	$31,000
economic growth:	8.4%
(2004)	

Consistent with its overall ageing trend, elderly women in Singapore will be a growing group in the coming decade. The fastest growing are women in elderly retired households, rising by an average of 7% a year to reach 195,000 in 2014, followed by working empty nesters at 4% to 517,800 in 2014. Women in young households will grow by only 0.6% a year to reach 619,000 in 2014. The middle aged women with children households are expected to be the slowest growing, at 0.5% a year. Some 279,000 women will be in this group by 2014. All Singaporeans are living longer. The average life expectancy is 78. However, this figure hides a major gender difference—only 84% of the men will live to see age 65, compared to 92% of the women.

Two groups stand out—women young singles and women working empty nesters. Both will be 350,000 strong by 2014, dwarfing all other groups. Both, in their own ways, are keen consumers driven by their lifestyles and they are the biggest discretionary spenders. By definition they have no children or dependent children at home, so they tend to focus their spending on themselves. In contrast, women in the married with children stage (the third largest, with 220,000 women expected by 2014) tend to spend mostly on their children.

Singapore's demographic shift has been taking place within an economic structural shift, with important implications for Singapore women as both producer and consumer. Unlike Hong Kong, Singapore has retained its significant manufacturing sector at about a quarter of the economy, as shown in Table 4.5.

Table 4.5
Different Paths of Change in Manufacturing

Manufacturing as % of economy	Hong Kong	Singapore
1985	21	23
1995	8	25
2003	5	25

(CEIC Data)

What has been changing in Singapore, however, is the manufacturing sector itself. Electronics assembling, the mainstay of Singapore's manufacturing sector in the 1980s and early 1990s, has been giving way to more technology- and knowledge-intensive health sciences and biomedical production. The growth of the electronic, chemical and biomedical production from 1999 to 2003 tells the story. From 1999, electronics and chemicals production grew a respectable 20%; but biomedical production soared 160%. Today this industry accounts for nearly one quarter of Singapore's manufacturing, up from nearly nothing at the start of the century.

This shift toward more skilled and knowledge-intensive manufacturing has benefited better-educated Singaporean women. As illustrated in Chart 4.5, not only are there more women working today compared with 10 years ago, but women's participation in the workforce today peaks between ages 25 to 29, the peak employment years for university educated and better-skilled women professionals.

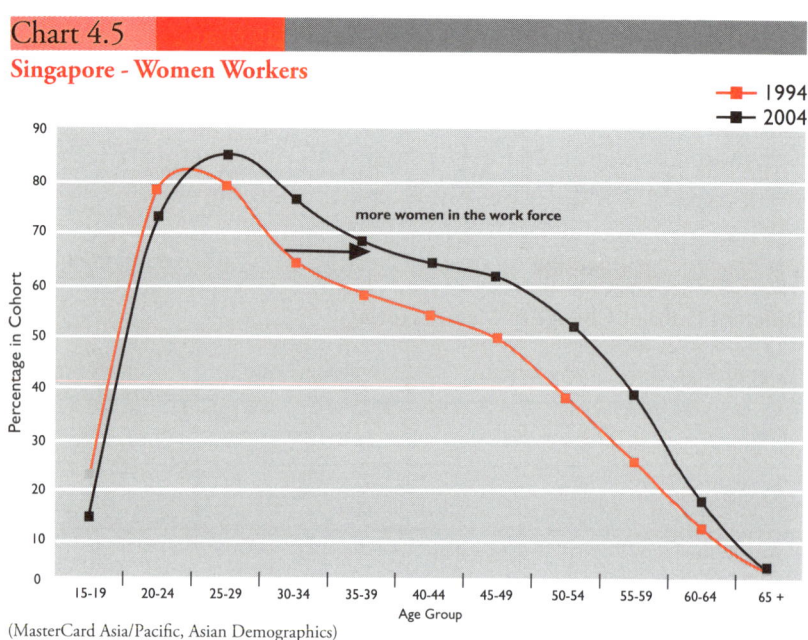

(MasterCard Asia/Pacific, Asian Demographics)

The structural shift in Singapore therefore works in a mutually reinforcing way with the demographic shift. As young women gain better education and jobs, they further delay marriage or opt to stay single. When married, they delay having children or opt to forgo children altogether. The net effect is that two powerful groups of women consumers are emerging—the young singles and the working empty nesters.

Looking at the four identified groups, the elderly retired households are estimated to grow the fastest, at 15%, in total spending over the next decade, boosting their spending power to $4 billion by 2014. The second fastest growing are the working empty nesters at 8% a year. By 2014, their total spending power will reach $12 billion. The young households (of which the young singles are a subset), come in third, with growth of 4%, and total spending power expected to be $11 billion in 2014. The middle aged married with children households will grow the slowest, at 3%, with total spending power in 2014 estimated at $8 billion.

Turning these figures into spending power per woman shows a different picture. Women in middle aged households have the highest spending, at almost $22,000 per woman, dwarfing young households at $13,800. In between are the empty nesters and elderly households, at $18,200 and $15,000 per woman respectively.

Table 4.6

SINGAPORE: Women Consumers: Potential Spending Power by Household

US$Billions ($2004)	2004	2014	Av. Annual Growth Rate
Young Households	$8.1	$11.0	3.60%
Middle Aged Households with Children	$5.8	$7.8	3.42%
Empty Nesters (working)	$7.0	$12.4	7.77%
Elderly Households (retired)	$1.7	$4.2	14.51%

(MasterCard Asia/Pacific, Asian Demographics)

The distribution and growth in discretionary spending are similar to those of total spending. Befitting their image as big spenders, by 2014, working empty nesters and young households will have the largest discretionary spending power, at $1.3 billion and $1.2 billion respectively. On an individual basis, however, middle aged households will have the highest discretionary spending, at $2,540 per woman. The empty nesters come next, at $2,100 per woman. The elderly and young households follow, with $1,760 and $1,600 per woman respectively.

Table 4.7

SINGAPORE: Women Consumers: Total Discretionary Expenditures by Household

US$Billions ($2004)	2004	2014	Av. Annual Growth Rate
Young Households	$0.9	$1.2	2.56%
Middle Aged Households with Children	$0.7	$0.8	2.38%
Empty Nesters (working)	$0.8	$1.3	6.41%
Elderly Households (retired)	$0.2	$0.4	12.62%

(MasterCard Asia/Pacific, Asian Demographics)

For discretionary spending, Singapore women, like their Hong Kong counterparts, like to dine out, followed by spending for transportation and communication, partially reflecting the high cost of owning a car in Singapore. Recreation and entertainment ranked third, followed by personal care, household purchases and health care.

Chart 4.6
SINGAPORE: Women Consumers: Key Discretionary Expenditures by Household Segments

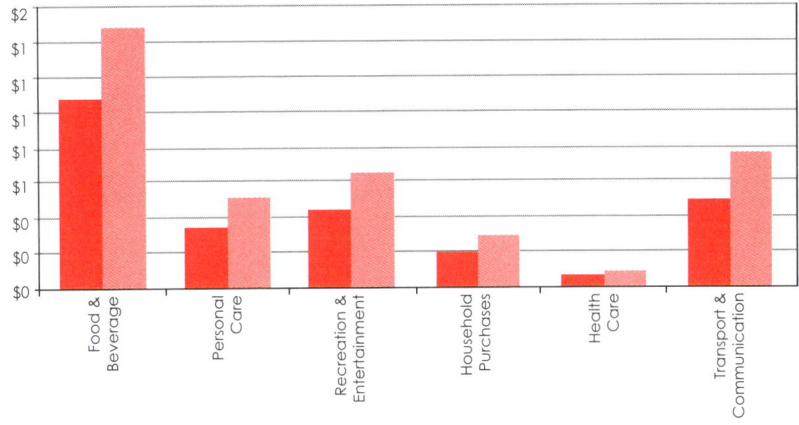

(MasterCard Asia/Pacific, Asian Demographics)

Understanding Singapore women's evolving lifestyles in an urban setting will be the key to success for business catering to their demand. In the coming decade, Singapore women consumers will be even better educated, more of them will have independent income and command significant household assets. Consistent with the ageing trend, elderly women will loom large in terms of their numbers and purchasing power. Understanding and meeting their needs will be a prerequisite of business success.

WOMEN CONSUMERS IN AFFLUENT ASIA: AUSTRALIA 5

AUSTRALIA

SNAPSHOT

population:	19 million
per capita income:	$33,000
economic growth:	3.2%
(2004)	

Australia is a developed country with about 19 million people, and a per capita income of roughly $33,000, putting it among the top in the world, and certainly among the most affluent countries in Asia. With its well-known progressive social policies, Australian women have long been well integrated into its economic life. The MasterIndex of Women's Advancement compiled by MasterCard in Asia, for example, shows that Australian women score very high on the objective scores of labor force participation and tertiary education (at 92.9). But their subjective scores are low, reflecting a much lower level of self-perception of their role in the work place (at 42.9).

In the coming decade, however, a convergence of demographic and economic trends will interact in dynamic ways to transform Australian women's role in the economy, and thereby their rising importance as consumers.

DEMOGRAPHICS DYNAMICS

Population growth has been slowing for some time in Australia. In the next decade, growth will average only 0.7% a year. At the same time, the population will also be ageing quickly. The group of those 40 and above will expand, while those below 14 will shrink.

Chart 5.1

A Slow Growing & Ageing Population: Australia Population Structure

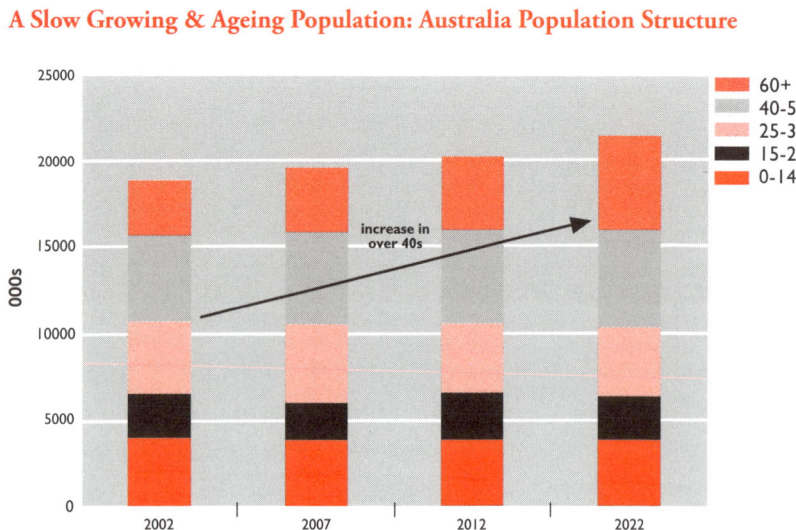

(MasterCard Asia/Pacific, Asian Demographics)

The ageing pattern, however, will differ between the sexes. As shown in Chart 5.2, women start to outnumber men at age 25. As they reach the age of 59 women will outnumber men by a large margin.

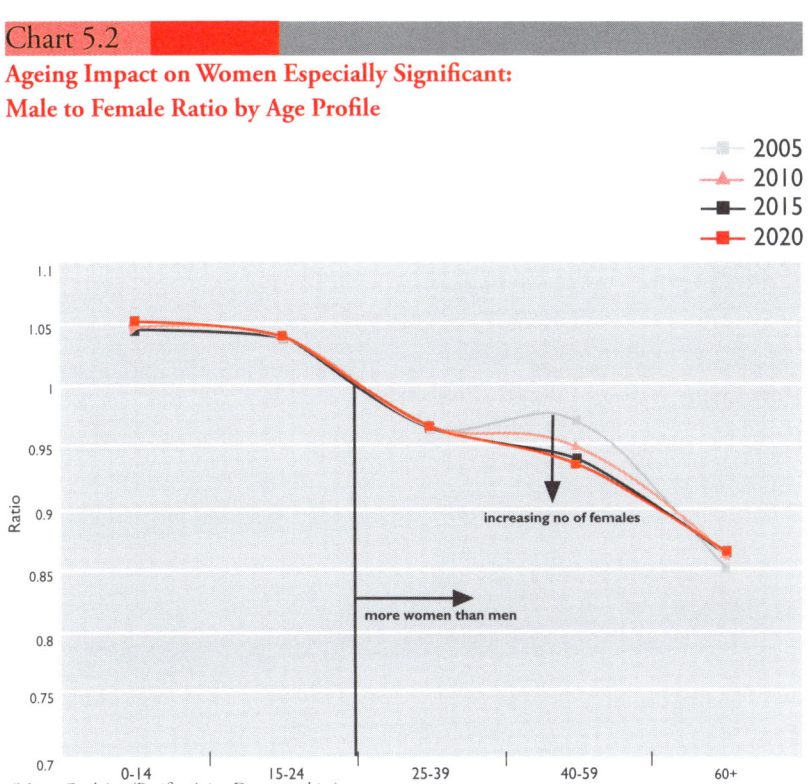

Chart 5.2
**Ageing Impact on Women Especially Significant:
Male to Female Ratio by Age Profile**

Compounding the ageing trend are fewer births. The number of live births per year will decline from 51 in 2002, to 48 in 2013 per thousand. In the next decade, about a quarter of Australian women are expected not to have any children at all. Thus the proportion of households without any dependent children—including households that have never had children and those whose children have left home—will rise from 61% now to 65% in 2013. So not only are Australian women having fewer babies, they are also postponing having them. There will be a lot more mothers in their 50s with very young children.

The combination of an ageing population and a delay in motherhood will fundamentally alter the distribution of households. The number of young marrieds with a child under the age of 10 will quite precipitously decline, while there will be a slight increase in the number of young marrieds with no kids and a significant rise in the number of older working age empty nesters and retired empty nesters (households without any dependent children). Households in the young singles' category will remain virtually unchanged. As a result, the pattern of household distribution will change from a multipeaks shape to a twin-peaks shape—bulging at the younger and older ends of the curve as shown in Chart 5.3.

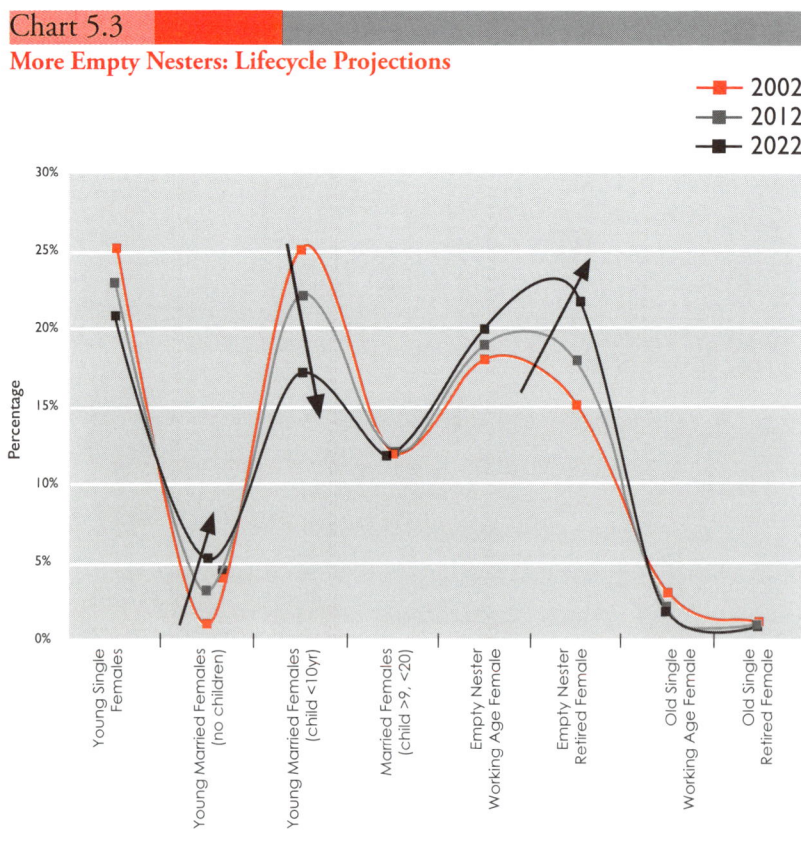

Chart 5.3
More Empty Nesters: Lifecycle Projections

(MasterCard Asia/Pacific, Asian Demographics)

Among the elderly, women will dominate. By 2012, for example, women will make up about 80% of the 70 to 74 years old group. In the coming decade, therefore, most old singles will be women. Overall, about five million baby boomers (born 1946 to 1964) will retire in the next decade, almost a quarter of the population. They control an estimated three quarters of total household assets in Australia. And, increasingly, women will dominate in these older groups which will have far-reaching implications for consumer markets in Australia.

ECONOMIC DYNAMICS

A conservative estimate of real growth of 2.3% a year for the next decade is used for projecting the size and composition of Australia's consumer market. The growth of the Australian economy has been put at around 3%, a relatively conservative rate. The Australian economy is changing. Traditional employment in the primary and manufacturing sectors is set to decline in the coming years, to be replaced by more jobs in the services. From a gender perspective, job opportunities for women should increase since they are overwhelmingly employed in the service sector.

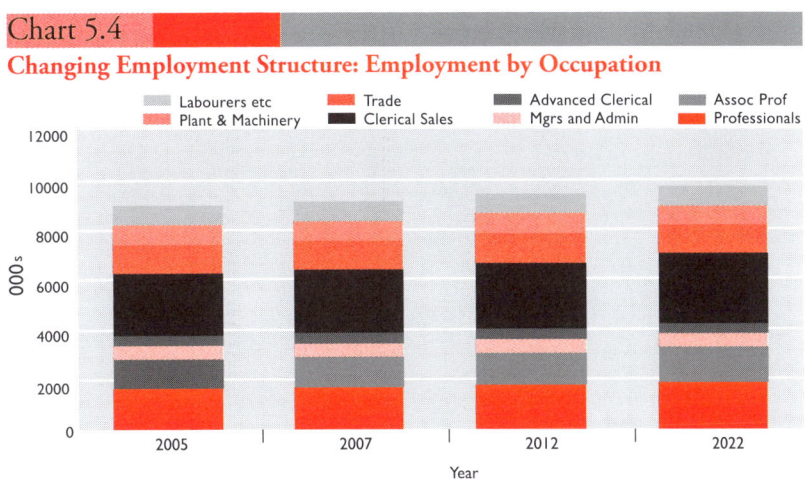

Chart 5.4
Changing Employment Structure: Employment by Occupation

(MasterCard Asia/Pacific, Asian Demographics)

Women's participation in the workforce, however, exhibits a unique pattern among developed societies—one which is "uniquely Australian." Most Australian women's priorities change when they become mothers. They believe they should stay home when their children are still of school age.[1] Most quit full-time employment and either stay home to look after the children, or seek part-time work. Some 71% of part-time workers in 2003 were women,[2] and they work mostly in the service sector. Thus, women's earning power has lagged behind that of men and their subjective perceptions—as revealed by the MasterIndex of Women's Advancement—of their positions at work (few believe they are in managerial positions) and their earning power (few believe they earn above-average income) have a basis in reality. The disparity between the sexes in their earnings within job categories is illustrated in Chart 5.5. Women on average earn about one tenth less than men with one interesting exception: "managers and administrators," where women earn more than men.

Chart 5.5

Women's Earning Power Has Lagged Behind: Ratio of Female to Male Earnings, 1999

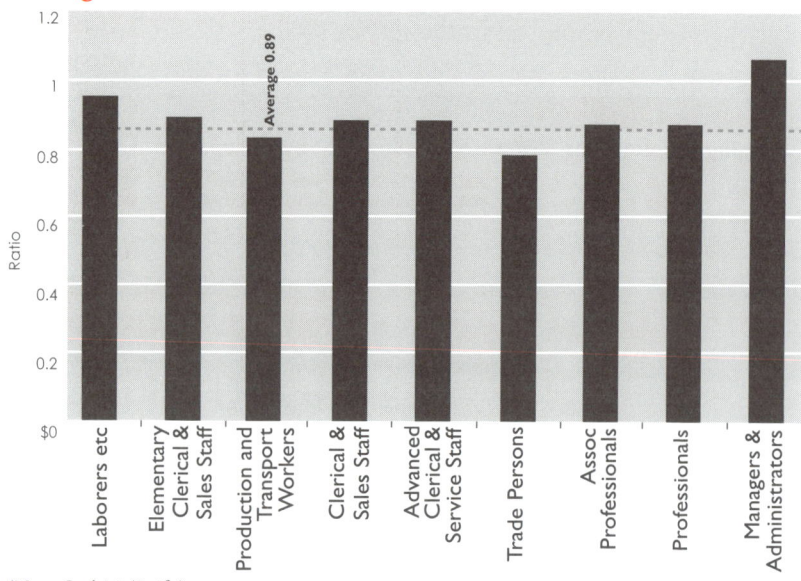

(MasterCard Asia/Pacific)

The expected change in the employment structure, however, will favor women since it is in services—women's traditional employment niche—that job growth will be the strongest. Growth is expected to be especially strong in service sectors such as wholesale and retail, community services, and finance and property.

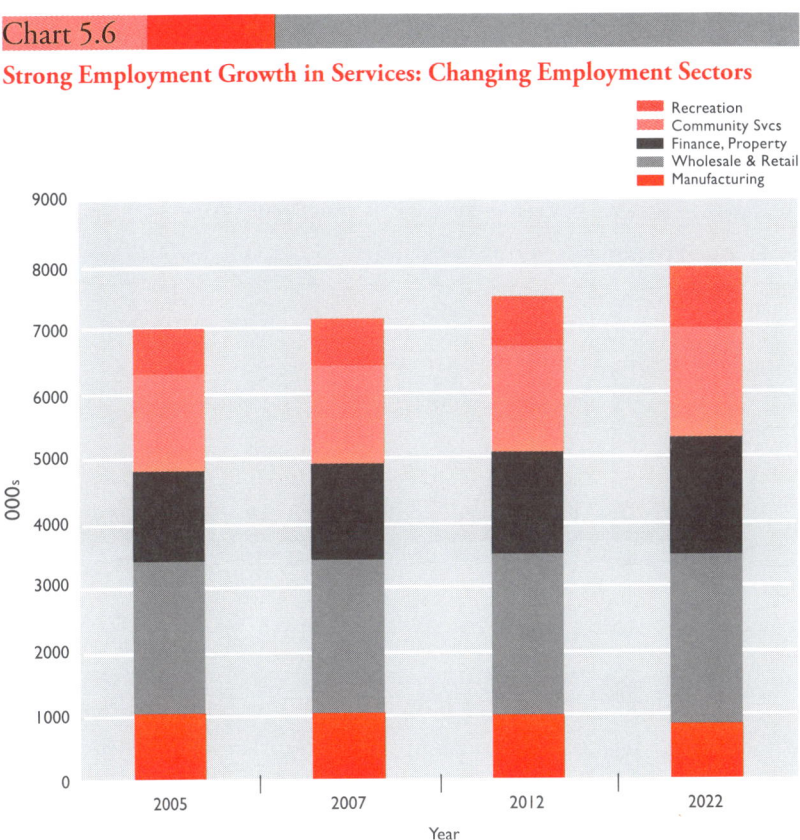

Chart 5.6
Strong Employment Growth in Services: Changing Employment Sectors

Women are more likely to have completed post-secondary education at the certificate level, whereas men tend to have more technical training. With the expected decline in job growth in the primary and manufacturing sectors and strong job growth in services, women's educational backgrounds should be more beneficial when compared with men's training in the trades.

Chart 5.7
Women Have More Post-Secondary Training: Educational Levels

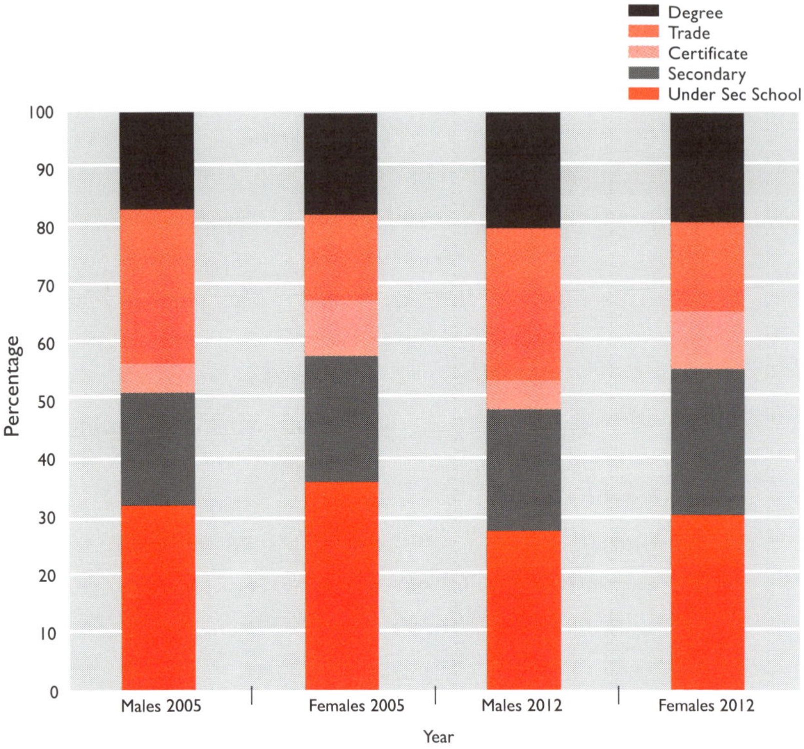

(MasterCard Asia/Pacific, Asian Demographics)

The implication of the changing economy is not just that there will be more service sector jobs, but more importantly the *type* of jobs are also changing. More service sector jobs will be in higher value-added areas and more knowledge intensive—and therefore better paid as well. With the increasing prevalence of mobile technology connectivity and innovations in the service sector, employment in the services will also become more flexible.

The line between full-time and part-time may blur—the issue will be more of getting the assigned tasks done within the required time frame, regardless of whether it is done by full-time or part-time staff. These two trends in service sector employment—higher value-added and flexibility—will allow Australian women to have their cake and eat it too, i.e., take care of children at home while suffering less employment disadvantage just because they disrupt their career path or opt for part-time (flexible) employment. This trend is, in fact, not new. It has been going on for some time as reflected by women's earning power rising faster than men's, especially among younger age groups. What is significant, perhaps, is the expectation that this trend will likely accelerate in the coming decade.

THE EVOLVING WOMEN CONSUMER MARKET IN AUSTRALIA

The convergence of these demographic and economic trends will shape the women consumer market in Australia in the next decade. As mentioned, the impact of ageing will be borne disproportionately by women—they simply live longer than men. Since the coming retirement generation of baby boomers is asset-rich, and as women continue to outlive men, much of these assets will be controlled by women in their 70s, 80s and 90s. Thus, despite their lower earning power, women will nevertheless have sufficient resources to support themselves in retirement. The following chart shows the pattern of the past: women depended more than men on government pension, but also on resources in the form of inheritance and spouses' pensions (represented by "others" and "other's income"), as well as their ability to continue to work part-time in some fashion. In the next decade, retirement resources for women represented by the "others" and "other's income" will increase significantly, so will their ability to continue to work part-time as they live longer, healthier and more active lives, and have more options in choosing when and how they want to retire or not to retire.

Chart 5.8
Women's Retirement Sources of Income in the Future Will Shift Significantly: Sources of Income in Retirement, 1997

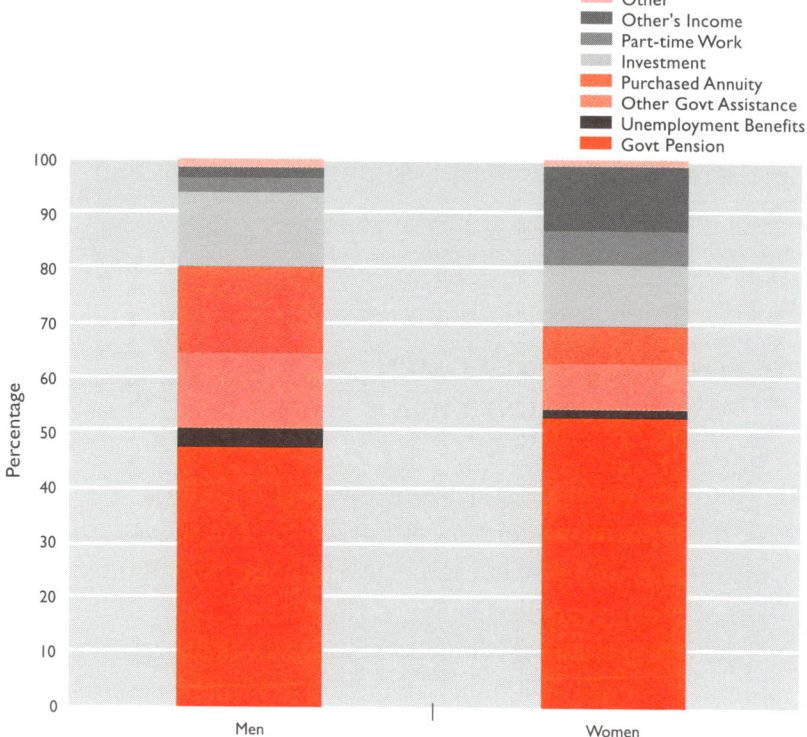

(MasterCard Asia/Pacific, Asian Demographics)

The women consumer market in the future will therefore be dominated by the younger and the older age groups. The younger women will increasingly benefit from the structural shift in the economy from manufacturing to services, enjoying better income than previous generations because services will become higher value-added. Younger women will also enjoy a more flexible employment arrangement where part-time work may not always mean lower pay and junior positions.

The older women will also dominate the consumer market as they live longer and healthier than ever before. A third group, the young marrieds with a child under 10, will also be relatively important.

Chart 5.9
The Women Consumer Market Will be Dominated by Young Singles & Empty Nesters: Women Consumer Estimated Market Size A$ bn

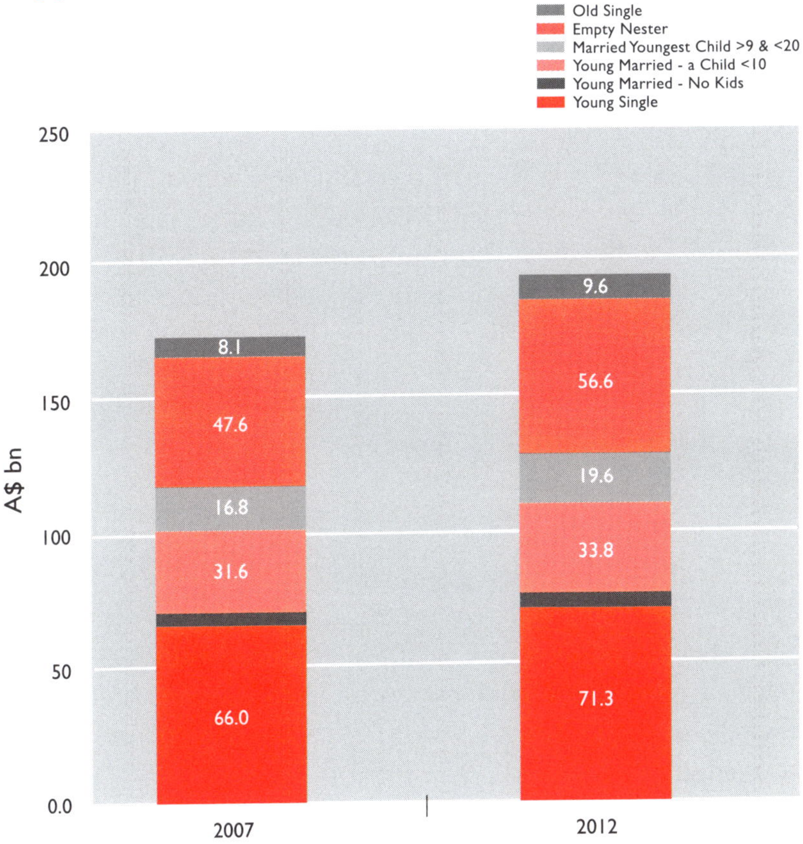

Legend:
- Old Single
- Empty Nester
- Married Youngest Child >9 & <20
- Young Married - a Child <10
- Young Married - No Kids
- Young Single

Segment	2007	2012
Old Single	8.1	9.6
Empty Nester	47.6	56.6
Married Youngest Child >9 & <20	16.8	19.6
Young Married - a Child <10	31.6	33.8
Young Single	66.0	71.3

(MasterCard Asia/Pacific, Asian Demographics)

The estimated total spending power of the four key women consumer groups is summarized in Table 5.1. Younger households have the biggest spending power of $52 billion, and are expected

Table 5.1
AUSTRALIA: Women Consumers: Potential Spending Power by Household

US$Billions ($2004)	2004	2014	Av. Annual Growth Rate
Young Households	$51.6	$57.4	1.11%
Middle Aged Households with Children	$22.7	$29.7	3.07%
Empty Nesters (working)	$27.9	$33.9	2.15%
Elderly Households (retired)	$20.5	$29.5	4.38%

(MasterCard Asia/Pacific, Asian Demographics)

to grow 1% a year in the next decade to $57 billion. Middle aged households, the third biggest, will grow at a higher rate of 3% and will have $30 billion of spending power in 2014. Working empty nesters, on the other hand, are the second biggest group, but will grow a bit more slowly than middle aged households, at 2% a year. In 2014, their spending power is projected to be $34 billion. It is elderly households that will have the highest growth, at 4%, with their spending power hitting $30 billion by 2014.

On a per women basis, however, it is the empty nesters that have the highest spending power at $17,300 per woman in 2004. While young households have the biggest spending power in total, their spending power is only $15,050 per woman, the lowest among the four groups. The middle age with children group and elderly households are in between, with $16,900 and $15,200 per woman respectively.

For discretionary spending, the overall pattern is similar for the four groups. Again, young households will have the biggest spending power; and elderly households will grow the fastest, at 4% a year, followed by middle aged households at 3%, working empty nesters households at 2% and young households at 1%.

On an individual basis, however, empty nesters have the highest discretionary spending, at $3,090 per woman, followed by middle aged households at $3,000 per woman, then elderly households at $2,700 per woman. Young households, in spite of discretionary spending power being the largest as a group, come last at $2,685 per woman.

Table 5.2
AUSTRALIA: Women Consumers: Total Discretionary Expenditures by Household

US$Billions ($2004)	2004	2014	Av. Annual Growth Rate
Young Households	$9.2	$10.3	1.13%
Middle Aged Households with Children	$4.0	$5.3	3.09%
Empty Nesters (working)	$5.0	$6.1	2.17%
Elderly Households (retired)	$3.7	$5.3	4.41%

(MasterCard Asia/Pacific, Asian Demographics)

Lifestyles will be of paramount importance in how these women spend their money, especially the younger and older age groups. Young singles, a subset of young households, will have high discretionary spending power as they tend to spend more on themselves, and save less as they postpone marriage and children. Older women will also have distinctive lifestyles. More active than previous generations, they will travel more and be more involved in recreational activities. Peer group activities among older women, as they form friendships among themselves, will also dominate. They will likely need more personal services, apart from health care, such as women-oriented wealth management and related financial services.

In spending patterns, recreation and entertainment will dominate and will be the fastest growing. This category is followed by food and beverage and transportation and communications. By 2014, these key expenditures will account for more than 40% of total women's discretionary spending.

Chart 5.10
AUSTRALIA: Women Consumers - Key Discretionary Expenditures by Household Segments

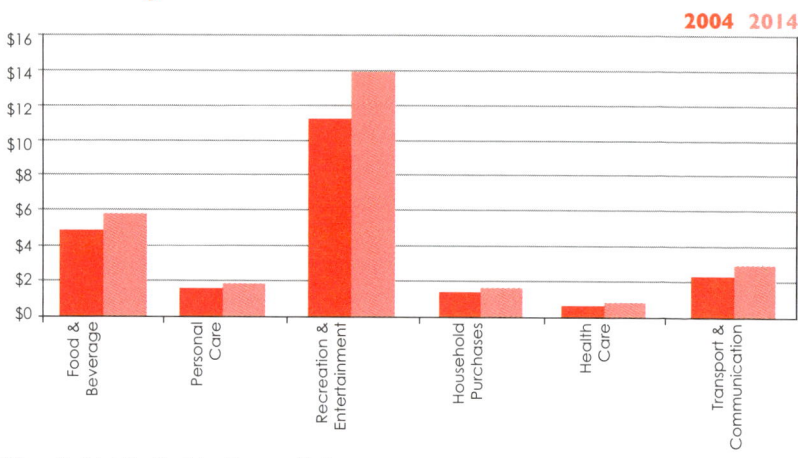

(MasterCard Asia/Pacific, Asian Demographics)

All these trends represent significant new business opportunities in the women consumer market. And if emerging young women's lifestyle trends need to be monitored and better understood, then those of older women must demand even more attention. The bottom line is that the women consumer market in Australia by 2014 will be a $150 billion market, growing at some 2.4% a year, higher than economic growth of about 1.6%.

WOMEN CONSUMERS IN EMERGING ASIA: CHINA   6

CHINA

SNAPSHOT

population:	1.3 billion
per capita income:	$1,300
economic growth:	10%
(2004)	

At close to 1.3 billion, China is the world's most populous country. Rapid economic growth has raised per capita income to close to $1,300 in 2004. China's high level of growth, excepting the inevitable volatility, is expected to continue for the foreseeable future. Its consumer market, given its size, growth momentum, and emerging segments of sophistication and high spending, is becoming more alluring everyday. China's consumer market is expected to be a powerhouse that will drive growth and business development in the coming decades. Analysis of key converging trends over a 10-year horizon, however, reveals that women consumers of China will emerge as a "powerhouse within the powerhouse" of China's consumer market. What China's women consumers will look like, what they will want and how they will consume are critical questions that businesses have to answer if they want to cater successfully to these consumers and benefit from their rising spending power.

The power of women consumers is closely related to their role as producers. To recap, China scores very high in the MasterIndex of Women Advancement with an overall index value of 80.7. The objective score, which averages women's labor force participation and tertiary education levels, is among the highest in the region (at 93.0). The subjective score, which reflects women's self-perceptions of their place in the workforce, is lower at 68.4; yet it is higher than that of Korea and Japan, which have higher per capita income. Thus women consumers in China are likely to have a strong "take-charge" attitude—more assertive and self-confident.

DEMOGRAPHIC SHOCK

Women's role in China's society and economy cannot be understood without examining the dramatic swings in China's population policies in the past half century. In the 1950s, China aggressively promoted large families to speed industrialization and enhance China's geopolitical clout. Birth rates rose dramatically and a huge population bulge appeared in the 1960s. Many of those who are now entering retirement come from that generation of runaway population growth. Women in that age group have suffered low living standards and poor education, all in the context of political turmoil and upheaval.

Runaway population growth was followed by a firm brake on fertility in the 1970s. A one-child policy was introduced in 1979 restricting families to one child each. But, paradoxically, a decline in fertility had actually started before then. The fertility rate plummeted from 5.3 in 1971, to 2.8 in 1978. Over two decades after the introduction of the policy, fertility declined to below replacement rate at 1.7 in 2004. Fertility is expected to continue its long-term decline in the coming decade.

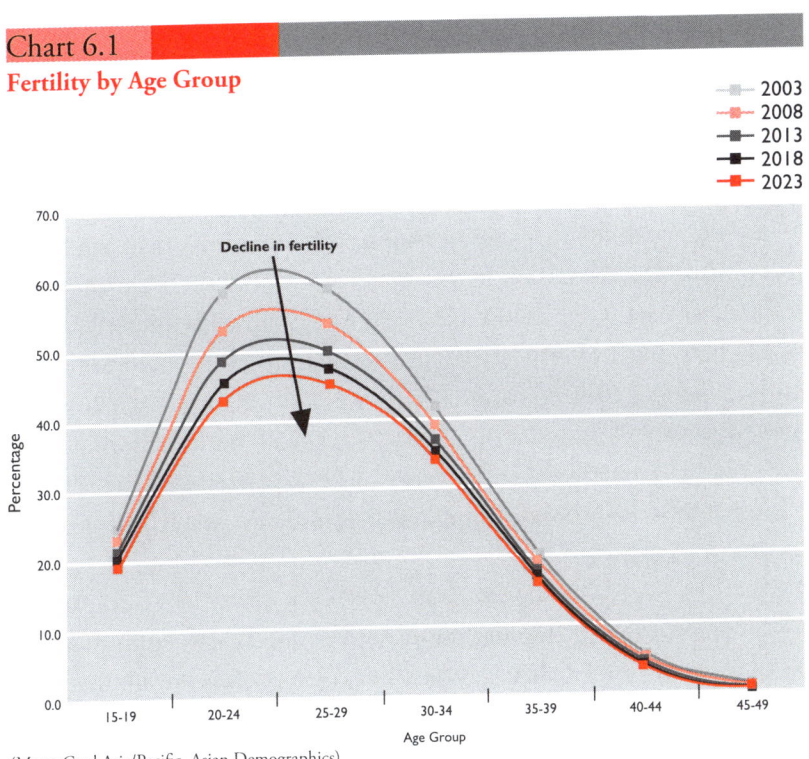

Chart 6.1
Fertility by Age Group

(MasterCard Asia/Pacific, Asian Demographics)

The result of this dramatic swing in population is nothing less than a demographic shock, with profound consequences for society and for Chinese women in particular. For example, the number of births in China is projected to decline from 11 million a year in 2003 to 6 million in 2023. Due to the traditional preference for male babies, and aided by sex-selective abortions, the male-to-female birth ratio in 2003 is estimated at around 118 male per 100 female births.

The overall population is set to peak soon. Precise estimates differ, but the consensus is that China's population will peak within the next decade and reach 1.35 billion by 2014, and will then go into a slow but steady decline. As an illustration of how significant a transition this is, it is projected that only 24 million people will be added to the population between 2003 and 2013, versus some 101 million added between 1992 and 2002.

Along with the peaking of the population is the rapid ageing of the population. In the next two decades, China will go from being a "middle aged" country to an older nation. The average age is 35 years old today. By 2023, it will be 45 years old. By then, the only country in Asia older than China will be Japan, with an average age of 47. To put it in perspective, consider that in 2000 there were 600 million people over 60 years of age worldwide, of whom roughly one fifth were Chinese. By 2020, there will be a billion people over 60 years old worldwide, and nearly a quarter of them will be Chinese. As women outlive men, increasingly this elderly group will be dominated by women.

The declining population growth is also a reflection of more young people opting to stay single and childless, or if married, postponing the start of a family. More couples are also opting not to have children at all. The one-child policy can be said to have succeeded all too well. Over one quarter of people aged 16 to 35 years planned to have no children at all, according to a survey conducted by the Youth League Committee of Beijing Municipality in 2001.

As a result, household formation in different lifecycle stages is set for dramatic changes in the next decade, which will directly affect consumption since households are the primary units of consumption. The shape, size and age of the household will effectively determine the expenditure by household members.

In 2003, young singles (under 35 years and not married), young married with no children (childless couples under 35 years) and married with a single child accounted for over three quarters of adults. By 2023, however, these households will have declined to only 43% of adults. On the other hand, the working age empty nesters (older working adults without any dependent children at home) and retired empty nesters (retired people without any dependent children at home) will account for 44% of the adult population.

With rapid population ageing and a social welfare system only at its infancy, how can the elderly care for themselves upon retirement when there are fewer working children and grandchildren to support them? Contrary to common belief, much of this older population, especially in the urban areas, will be financially well off.

One of the main reasons for this financial well-being is the same as that in many developed countries: a large pool of value in home ownership. Between 1999 and 2001 urban dwellers were made into property owners when the government sold them their dwellings at nominal prices. Previously, all urban residents of China had had to rent a flat from their work units or from the government. Nobody owned private homes. Then, virtually overnight, China's urban residents became property owners. Though largely ignored by the media, this was arguably the largest wealth transfer in history, and it positively affected some 460 million urban residents of China.

With the opening up of the secondary housing market, many of these home owners can now sell these flats at multiples of what they paid, and then use the proceeds as down payments for more upmarket private condominiums. The privatization of the housing market, while boosting the rapid expansion of the middle class, has also provided significant added household assets for middle aged people to finance their retirement in the coming decade. Many older women will be such beneficiaries.

SOCIAL TRANSFORMATION

Since the founding of the People's Republic in 1949, the government's ideology regarding women has been one of full equality with men. Inevitably there are gaps between rhetoric and reality. But much of the rhetoric has turned out to be true. Official statistics report that women account for about half the workforce and their pay is about 80% that of men. Around a third of senior government officials are women, and women held one fifth of the seats in the National People's Congress in 2002. Women remain, however, a rarity at the apex of political and economic power, with only one female member in the Politburo.

The status of women in China in the coming decade will be affected by three critical trends: urbanization, education and expansion of the manufacturing sector. The rapid expansion of the manufacturing sector has been particularly important as young women with only a high school education or less have flooded the workforce, to take jobs in all the new manufacturing industries. In most labor intensive industries such as garments, shoes and textiles, the workforce consists almost entirely of women. For example, in Shenzhen, China's southern manufacturing hub, women outnumber men in the work force. In 2002, four million of the five million workers in Shenzhen were women.

China's manufacturing sector is expected to expand in the next decade. As labor costs rise in the coastal region, labor intensive manufacturing has started to move inland. The average wage in Sichuan, for example, is only one third that of the Greater Shanghai region. The government's massive investment in transport and communications infrastructure has helped spur this inland migration. With improved accessibility, the interior is being connected to the major commercial and service hubs such as Shanghai and Beijing. Labor demand for less educated and less skilled women in the manufacturing sector will increase in the interior provinces in the next decade.

At the opposite end of the spectrum, the emergence of a megacity such as Shanghai is creating strong demand for educated and skilled professionals and knowledge workers. While exact data are unavailable, anecdotal evidence suggests that well educated women are increasingly successful in their careers.

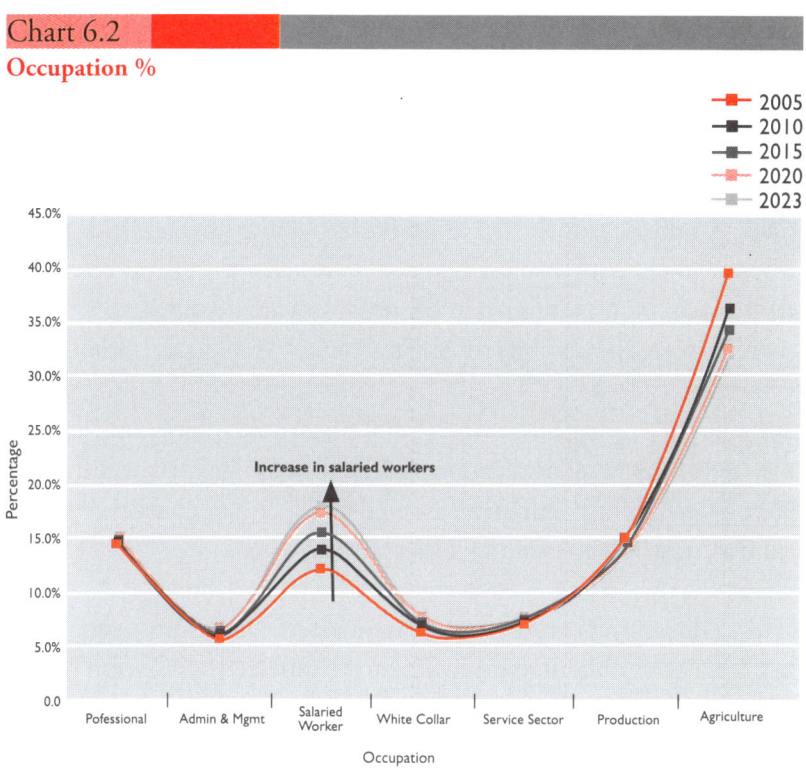

Chart 6.2
Occupation %

(MasterCard Asia/Pacific, Asian Demographics)

Urbanization is a fast growing trend in China. In recent years, between 15 and 20 million people were urbanized per year, both from rural migration as well as rural areas being "urbanized" through infrastructure development and the amalgamation of rural centers into urban hubs. This trend is expected to continue for the foreseeable future. By 2023, two thirds of the population will be urbanized.

This has huge socioeconomic implications. While many people in rural areas are underemployed and productivity is low, urban workers tend to have higher and more productive employment. Their earning power is correspondingly much higher. Provincial capitals, for example, accounted for 9% of the total population in 2003, but a third of total income. While the economic benefits of urbanization apply to both men and women, for women there are additional benefits. In the rural areas, traditional practices that value men over women have persisted, in spite of decades of ideological campaigns by the government.

An urban culture, however, means a more liberated culture for women, everything else being equal. Women's social and economic mobility is much stronger in an urban setting, even if there is no change in traditional beliefs in rural areas. Thus urban households will soon exceed the number of rural households (these urban households will be smaller than rural households, however), even as the size of the rural population will be much bigger than the urban population. Many urban households will either consist of single women or will be headed by older women.

Education is an important "equalizer," and this is just as true in China as anywhere else. However, the impact of education is even more powerful in China because of the rapid decline in population growth. The number of school-age children will drop from 283 million in 2003 to about 129 million in 2023. This shrinking of the school-age population means that there will be an accelerated increase in education resources per school-age child. Even as the quantity of education is increasing for students, the quality of education will also be improved simultaneously.

The number of poorly educated (with only primary school education) will decline from 27% of the population over 15 years of age in 2008 to 10% in 2018. Correspondingly, in the same period, the number of those with junior high school education will rise from 43% to 55%, and the number of those with university education from 8% to 12%. The expansion of higher education and improvement in the quality of education will therefore benefit younger Chinese women greatly in the coming decade.

WOMEN CONSUMERS OF CHINA

The convergence of employment opportunities, with more and better education for women, will be most powerfully felt within the fast-expanding urban setting. The emerging Chinese women consumers will be found mostly in urban areas. Women in cities have more economic freedom and choice, and greater financial and social independence.

A survey[1] conducted in 2000, estimated that some 85% of working age urban Chinese women had their own sources of income, even if married and even if their husbands earned enough to support the family. And there is evidence that women are assuming a more proactive role in planning and managing family finances. About half of the women said they had a bigger say in family finances than ever before.

Chinese households are becoming more accustomed to the concept of credit. In the same 2000 survey, only 27% of heads of households reported that they did not like the idea of buying on credit, down from 53% five years ago. The majority of the respondents either had used or would like to use consumer credit and loans. About half of the respondents also reported holding bonds and stocks as investments along with the traditional savings deposits, a major shift from the time when people had all their savings in bank accounts and paid cash for virtually everything.

As the trend of delayed marriage or staying single continues, the size of the household is shrinking. The number of households with two persons or less is rising fast. It is expected that they will grow to 216 million in 2023, from 104 million in 2003. Within these households, the segment headed by middle aged householders (40 to 59 years) will be the fastest growing. It is projected to increase by one-third in 10 years' time.

The combination of changing age, size, tastes and income of China's urban households will entail dramatic changes in how the people in these households live their lives and how they spend their money. These changes are reflected in a number of urban lifestyles that have emerged in recent years. The first are the urban young singles. They were the children of the first one-child policy generation, born in the late 1970s and entering adulthood now. As the single child, each grew up in a high stress environment, pampered by two parents and four grandparents. Studies have shown that they are more health conscious than their parents, and are keen consumers of health care services and the fitness industry. It is estimated that they spend around 10% of their disposable income on health and fitness-related services.

A related lifestyle trend of this generation is that they enjoy travel. It has become fashionable for them to organize trips themselves, (doing research on the internet and planning their own trips) for both domestic and overseas travel. Along with their enthusiasm for travel, their overall lifestyle is that of an urban youth—they spend almost all their disposable income on themselves. As they don't need to support their parents who are still working, they can spend on clothing, dining out, travel, fitness, and other urban entertainment and leisure activities.

The young singles, especially young single women, carry their singles lifestyle into their married lives. A Chinese version of DINK (double income, no kids), is estimated to account for 10% of families in large urban areas. A 2004 survey[2] found that since 1997 the number of couples in Beijing, Shanghai, Guangzhou and Wuhan opting for a DINK lifestyle has been on the increase. Preference for the DINK lifestyle is also found to correlate with income—over 14% aspire to the DINK lifestyle among those earning more than 5,000 yuan (roughly $600) per month, whereas only 6% do so among those earning less than 5,000 yuan per month. The leading sociologist Li Yinhe has observed that DINKs "are mostly hedonists who value individuality and the quality of married life more than parenthood."

One version of the DINK couple is the "A-A" couple. In an A-A couple, both partners control their own disposable incomes. All bills are strictly divided. So A-A couples enjoy the benefits of cohabitation, but retain their financial independence. A-A couples tend to be young, comparatively wealthy, and exclusively urban. A-A couples first appeared in the coastal cities of Guangdong Province, and have since spread to other urban centers. A minority of the A-A couples are actually not married. It remains to be seen whether A-A couples will establish themselves as a social institution, or whether they are just a passing phase.

Another emerging young urban lifestyle is the rise of the so called "F-Generation." They are reminiscent of the hippy culture in the West in the 1960s. Members of the F-generation are very young, in their late teens and early 20s, and have neither career nor stable income. Many don't seem to have permanent dwellings either. Most of them are well educated and technologically savvy, brought up in a typical middle-class urban family. They have opted to pursue more idealistic and intellectual goals, turning away from monetary incentives.[3] Though a fringe phenomenon at present, it may well become more popular over time with rising prosperity.

Women figure prominently in all these new urban lifestyles. Many young women are, of course, first generation children of the one-child policy generation. Many are well educated, with professional careers and have opted for a young single's lifestyle. The really independent-minded are those who have formed A-A couples even after marriage. Assertive and confident young women are also prominent among the fringe phenomenon of the F-Generation.

Opposite from the young and single lifestyles of urban women are the older segments, grouped into empty nesters and old singles. The empty nesters are those over 45, still married, but without dependent children. The old singles are similar to the empty nesters, except that they are widows or widowers, and mostly retired. In a strange mirror image to the young singles and DINKs, the empty nesters and old singles are increasingly living independent, healthy and active lives. And they are living longer as well. For those with sufficient financial assets, they tend to spend money on themselves, pursuing their personal interests and hobbies with close friends and companions.

In size, estimates of urban female population in the lifecycle stages are in Table 6.1 for 2008 and 2013.

The size of the different groups between 2008 and 2013 is a reflection of the overall ageing trend. Young singles maintain its size largely due to more people staying single in spite of the overall shrinkage of the group. While the size of young married households will decline, those of the empty nesters and elderly households are set to rise.

Table 6.1
Dramatic Decline in Fertility

	2008 (million)	2013 (million)
Young Singles (under 35 not married)	28	27
Young Married (one child under 10)	43	32
Middle Aged Married (with child 10 - 20)	67	63
Empty Nesters	63	78
Elderly Households (old singles)	22	28

(MasterCard Asia/Pacific, Asian Demographics)

The corresponding spending power of women in each stage is estimated for 2004 and 2014. Calculated in constant 2004 US dollars, the total spending power of empty nesters and elderly households is projected to grow strongly at 15% and 11% a year in the next decade. By 2014, the women empty nesters and elderly households will have $245 billion and $112 billion, respectively, of spending power, compared with $259 billion for young households and $178 billion for middle aged married households.

Individually, however, the pattern looks different. The empty nesters had the largest spending power in 2004 at $1,020 per woman; and they are expected to retain their lead in the next decade, when their spending power is projected to be $1,540 in 2014. In 2014, women in middle aged households will be close behind with a spending power of $1,500. Elderly households will be next, at $930 per woman. Young households will have the lowest individual spending power, at $750 per woman in 2014.

Table 6.2
CHINA: Women Consumers: Potential Spending Power by Household

US$Billions ($2004)	2004	2014	Av. Annual Growth Rate
Young Households	$180.3	$259.1	4.37%
Middle Aged Households with Children	$110.8	$177.7	6.04%
Empty Nesters (working)	$100.0	$244.6	14.45%
Elderly Households (retired)	$54.3	$112.2	10.67%

(MasterCard Asia/Pacific, Asian Demographics)

Reflecting their increasingly affluent lifestyles, Chinese women consumers will be spending less on basics, and more on discretionary items and services. Empty nesters households will have the fastest growing discretionary spending power in the next decade, growing 16% a year. By 2014, these households will command $43 billion of discretionary spending power. The second fastest growing segment is the elderly households at 8%, but their actual discretionary spending power will be small, estimated at $2 billion. Young households, of which young singles are a subset, will see their discretionary spending power grow the slowest, at 5% a year. But they will have the most to spend on discretionary items and services, estimated to reach $45 billion in 2014. The discretionary spending power of the middle aged households will grow slightly faster than young households, at 7% a year, and will have $31 billion at their disposal by 2014.

As in the case of total spending, on an individual basis discretionary spending power looks very different. Empty nesters have the highest discretionary spending, at $170 per woman, next is middle aged households at $160 per woman. Young households are the second lowest, at $125 per woman. Finally, at $14 per woman, elderly households do not appear to have any discretionary spending at all. Apart from the change in the ranking of the four household groups in spending power, it should also be noted that individual spending power is still very low in China, in spite of its large aggregate numbers at the household levels.

Table 6.3
CHINA - Women Consumers: Total Discretionary Expenditures by Household

US$Billions ($2004)	2004	2014	Av. Annual Growth Rate
Young Households	$30.1	$45.2	5.00%
Middle Aged Households with Children	$18.5	$31.0	6.75%
Empty Nesters (working)	$16.7	$42.7	15.53%
Elderly Households (retired)	$0.8	$1.5	8.39%

(MasterCard Asia/Pacific, Asian Demographics)

The biggest and fastest rising discretionary expenditures are recreation and entertainment, and food and beverage, followed by transportation and communication, and personal care. The urban women consumers will be spending much of their hard-earned cash on personal travel and related cultural and recreational activities, dining out, shopping, as well as buying cars and pursuing urban leisure lifestyles.

As shown in Chart 6.3, on a per capita basis discretionary spending will remain low in the next 10 years. Within each of the age segments, discretionary spending will be found in geographic and social clusters with high incomes and consumer oriented lifestyles. The business challenge is to locate these clusters and effectively access them with the right products, competitive prices and brand appeal.

Chart 6.3
CHINA: Women Consumers - Key Discretionary Expenditures by Household Segment

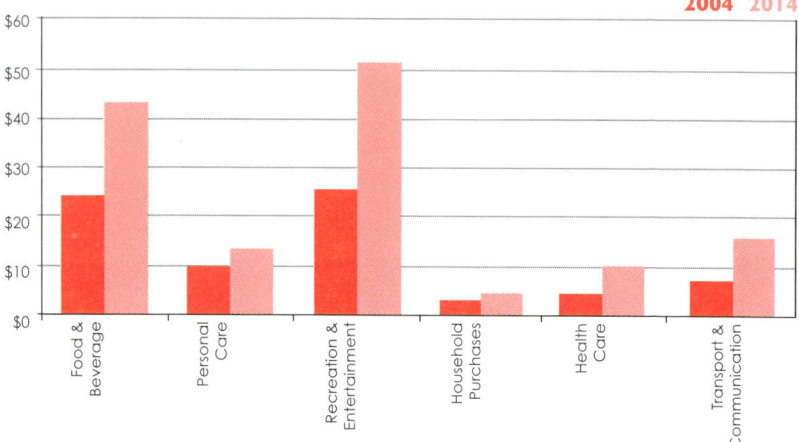

(MasterCard Asia/Pacific, Asian Demographics)

WOMEN CONSUMERS IN EMERGING ASIA: INDIA, MALAYSIA, THE PHILIPPINES & THAILAND

7

The four emerging markets in this chapter are a diverse group in size, income level and growth dynamics. Like most Asian emerging markets, they are rapidly evolving economies. While specific drivers of growth differ among them, women consumers are poised to become an increasingly important market in all four countries.

INDIA

SNAPSHOT

population:	1 billion
per capita income:	$640
economic growth:	7.1%
(2004)	

Not surprisingly, India has one of the youngest populations in Asia. Among the major regional markets, only the Philippines and Vietnam have younger populations. But compared to China, India has some 75 million more children. Population growth in India, however, has been slowing. Average growth for the next decade is expected to be 1.5% a year, down from the 1.8% a year of the last decade. The average age in India today is about 26, rising slowly to 28 by 2014.

Women have seen a steady improvement in education in recent years. In 1995, only 73% of Indian women were functionally literate. In 2004, the figure had risen to 79%. And by 2014, some 88% of women will be functionally literate. These averages, however, hide a significant gap between urban and rural women. Needless to say, rural women lag behind in education, and are 70% of the total female population. Currently only half of rural women are functionally literate, compared with 85% for urban women. While the situation is improving for rural women, the pace is slower. Close to 70% of rural women will be literate within a decade, but it will still be much lower than the estimated 90% in urban areas.

Significant gaps are also found in income levels between urban and rural households. The average annual income of an urban household was $3,540 in 2004. With an average household of five people, this results in $708 per capita. In contrast, the average rural household income is $1,300 annually, and the average household is six people, making per capita income a much lower $217.

Affluent households, defined as those earning $15,000 or more, are found mostly in urban areas. Today there are 561,000 households in this category, and by 2014, the number is expected to be over 1.2 million. For labor force participation, the women's rate is still low. Only a quarter of women are working, a figure that is expected to change little over the decade. However, these estimates cover only the so-called formal sector. In villages most able-bodied women work in some way and may even contribute more than rural men. A detailed breakdown of the labor force participation by age and gender is unavailable. But younger women in urban areas are obviously better educated, and these women are active in the labor force. In the tech sector, for example, women's participation rate can be assumed to be much higher, if not actually at parity with men.

Given the youthfulness of the population, it is unsurprising that young households, which comprise young singles, young married with no children and young married with a child under the age of nine, account for the lion's share of women's total spending power. These young women command some $92 billion of spending power, a figure that will grow by 5% a year to 2014 to reach $136 billion.

The spending patterns of young households are, however, likely to differ between the lifecycle stages. Young single women, found predominantly in urban areas, are like their counterparts anywhere else. They spend money on themselves, and follow the latest trends. The young marrieds without children, a small subset of this group (Indian women tend to have children quickly once married), tend to spend less and save more as they expect to have children soon. For those who do not plan to have children, again a rare situation, their spending pattern would be similar to young singles. For the young marrieds, their spending is tied to the needs of their growing families.

Women in middle aged with children households have the second largest purse, collectively controlling $47 billion of spending power. Growing at 10% a year, their spending power should reach $92 billion by 2014. The empty nesters, working couples with no dependent children, have a total spending power of $12 billion.

Their spending power will also grow at 10% a year, which will increase their spending power to $24 billion by 2014.

Retired elderly households, at the other end of the spectrum from young households, have the least spending power, about $11 billion but this will grow to reach $19 billion by 2014. On an individual basis, however, middle aged with children households have the highest spending power at $550 per woman. Empty nesters come next at $478 per woman. Elderly households follow with $449 per woman. Young households have the lowest spending power at $429 per woman.

Table 7.1
INDIA: Women Consumers - Potential Spending Power by Household

US$Billions ($2004)	2004	2014	Av. Annual Growth Rate
Young Households	$92.2	$136.2	4.76%
Middle Aged Households with Children	$46.8	$91.7	9.60%
Empty Nesters (working)	$11.8	$24.0	10.42%
Elderly Households (retired)	$11.0	$18.8	7.11%

(MasterCard Asia/Pacific, Asian Demographics)

Discretionary expenditure is quite low, as households spend most of their money on basic necessities. Young households, because of their lifestyle orientation, spend the most with a total discretionary spending of $92 billion in 2004. With some 225 million women in this group, it means their average spending is about $86 per person per year. The expected growth of their discretionary spending, however, will not be that high at 6% a year because of the high base from which it is projected. In 2014, their individual discretionary spending should reach $120 per woman, the highest among the four groups.

In middle aged households, women commanded $6 billion of discretionary spending power in 2004. For the 85 million women in this group, each has $66 in discretionary spend per year. Growing at 9.6% per year, their total discretionary spending should be $10.4 billion by 2014, or $107 per woman. For empty nesters, total discretionary spending was only $2 billion in 2004, or about $72 per woman per year. But they will have the highest growth rate at 10.4% a year. Their total discretionary spending will reach $4 billion by 2014, or $92 per woman a year.

Finally, for women in retired elderly households, their discretionary spending was the lowest in 2004 at $1 billion, or $52 per woman and the expected growth is also low at about 8%. Their total discretionary spending will be only $2 billion by 2014, or $68 per woman.

Table 7.2
INDIA: Women Consumers - Total Discretionary Expenditures by Household

US$Billions ($2004)	2004	2014	Av. Annual Growth Rate
Young Households	$18.8	$29.9	6.25%
Middle Aged Households with Children	$5.6	$11.0	9.64%
Empty Nesters (working)	$1.8	$3.6	10.00%
Elderly Households (retired)	$1.3	$2.3	7.69%

(MasterCard Asia/Pacific, Asian Demographics)

Similar to China, the large spending power in total translates into small spending power on individual levels, reflecting the low overall per capita income. The discretionary spending per woman is even lower as most households must spend the majority of their disposable income on basic necessities. Women in young households stand out in that they have the highest discretionary spending individually in both absolute terms as well as a percentage of their total spending power.

Patterns of spending on discretionary items are expected to change over the next decade, with recreation and entertainment (including the fast-rising personal travel category) becoming the biggest segment, replacing food and beverage as the biggest item. This change is a direct reflection of the increasing affluence of urban households.

Chart 7.1

INDIA: Women Consumers - Key Discretionary Expenditures by Household Segment

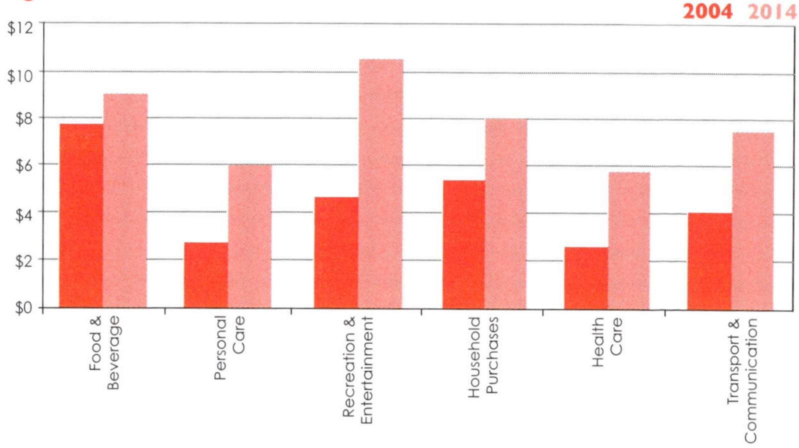

2004 2014

Category	2004	2014
Food & Beverage	$7.7	$9.0
Personal Care	$2.7	$6.0
Recreation & Entertainment	$4.6	$10.5
Household Purchases	$5.3	$7.9
Health Care	$2.5	$5.6
Transport & Communication	$3.9	$7.3

(MasterCard Asia/Pacific, Asian Demographics)

MALAYSIA

SNAPSHOT

population: 25 million
per capita income: $5,000
economic growth: 7.2%
(2004)

Malaysia's population is almost as young as India's. In 2004 the average age was 27, and by 2014 it will increase to 32. Persistent cultural bias in favor of boys has resulted in there being slightly more men than women in the population—49% women versus 51% men. As the population is still young, the longer life expectancy of women has yet to make its impact felt. In the coming decade, however, women's longer life expectancy will slowly adjust the gender ratio in the population, bringing it closer to parity. Malaysian women today have a life expectancy of 82 years, versus 74 for men.

With rapid urbanization, better education and career opportunities for women, the fertility rate of Malaysian women has declined quite significantly in recent years. In the early 1970s, for example, the average Malaysian woman had more than five children. These days it is about three.

Virtually all Malaysian women are literate (96%) and about three quarters of them complete secondary education. These averages hide significant gaps between urban and rural women, between the different ethnic groups with women in urban areas being more literate and better educated, as well as between women in Chinese or Indian families, versus those from pure Malay families. At 45%, the women's labor force participation rate is quite low, especially when compared to men's labor force participation of 80%. Again, given their better education, women from Chinese and Indian families are basically just as active in the labor force as men.

In recent years, the growth of manufacturing, now dominated by the electronics industry, has been slowing. Growth in services, in contrast, has been much faster. Financial and personal services, wholesale and retail, hospitality services have all rapidly expanded. For educated women, employment opportunities have become more diverse and abundant, especially in urban areas. This long-term structural shift in the economy is expected to continue for the foreseeable future. Consequently, the job market will continue to favor women who are well educated and highly skilled. In the coming decade, working women's income will rise strongly, in turn making them more important as consumers.

For the broad household segments, the young households have the biggest purse with total spending at $16 billion. Their spending is expected to grow at over 5% a year to reach $24 billion by 2014. The middle aged married with children households are next with $9 billion of spending power and that is growing at 7% a year to reach an estimated $15 billion by 2014. Both the empty nesters and the elderly households have much smaller spending power, estimated at $3 billion and $2 billion respectively in 2004. But both will see their spending power grow very fast at over 10% a year in the next decade.

Individually, it is the middle aged households that have the biggest spending power, at $4,500 per women. They are expected to keep their top position in 2014, at $5,880 per woman. Elderly households come next, at $3,950 per women, followed by the empty nesters, at $3,300 per woman. By 2014, however, empty nesters will overtake elderly households to become number two, with $5,100 per woman, compared with the latter's $4,500 per woman. Young households, in contrast, had the lowest individual spending power, at $2,900 in 2004, and this will increase to an estimated $3,900 by 2014.

Table 7.3

MALAYSIA: Women Consumers: Potential Spending Power by Household

US$Billions ($2004)	2004	2014	Av. Annual Growth Rate
Young Households	$15.7	$24.0	5.25%
Middle Aged Households with Children	$8.6	$14.7	7.08%
Empty Nesters (working)	$2.9	$6.0	10.69%
Elderly Households (retired)	$1.9	$4.0	10.78%

(MasterCard Asia/Pacific, Asian Demographics)

Discretionary spending among the four groups is largely similar to that of total spending. As summarized in Table 7.4, young households dominate, followed by middle aged with children, then empty nesters, with elderly households finishing last. On an individual basis, the picture looks different. Instead of young households, the middle age with children group leads, at $421 per woman. Surprisingly, elderly households come in second, at $412 per woman. The empty nesters rank third, at $342 per woman, while young households are the lowest, at $279 per woman. All four groups' discretionary spending will grow strongly in the next decade. Their ranking will remain unchanged, with the highest discretionary spending per woman to be found in the middle age group, at $524 in 2014, followed by the elderly households, at $454 per woman, then empty nesters, at $425 per woman. For the young households, it will be $355 per woman.

Table 7.4
MALAYSIA: Women Consumers - Total Discretionary Expenditures by Household

US$Billions ($2004)	2004	2014	Av. Annual Growth Rate
Young Households	$1.5	$2.2	4.72%
Middle Aged Households with Children	$0.8	$1.3	6.49%
Empty Nesters (working)	$0.3	$0.5	9.98%
Elderly Households (retired)	$0.2	$0.4	10.07%

(MasterCard Asia/Pacific, Asian Demographics)

Of the major items of their discretionary spending, food and beverage are the most important, which means dining out is a favorite activity. Next in importance are recreation and entertainment, and transportation and communication. The former is likely to be driven by the rising trend of personal travel, whereas the latter by an increase in car ownership.

It is worth remembering that Malaysia's working women are confident and self-assured. Their subjective score in the MasterIndex of Women's Advancement is an impressive 100.9, the highest among all the countries surveyed. The score means that for every 100 Malaysian men who believed in 2004 that they were in a managerial position and earned above-average income, 100.9 Malaysian women believed the same. Clearly this level of confidence would contribute to their assertiveness and willingness to experiment as consumers, making theirs a truly dynamic market segment.

Chart 7.2
MALAYSIA: Women Consumers - Key Discretionary Expenditures by Household Segment

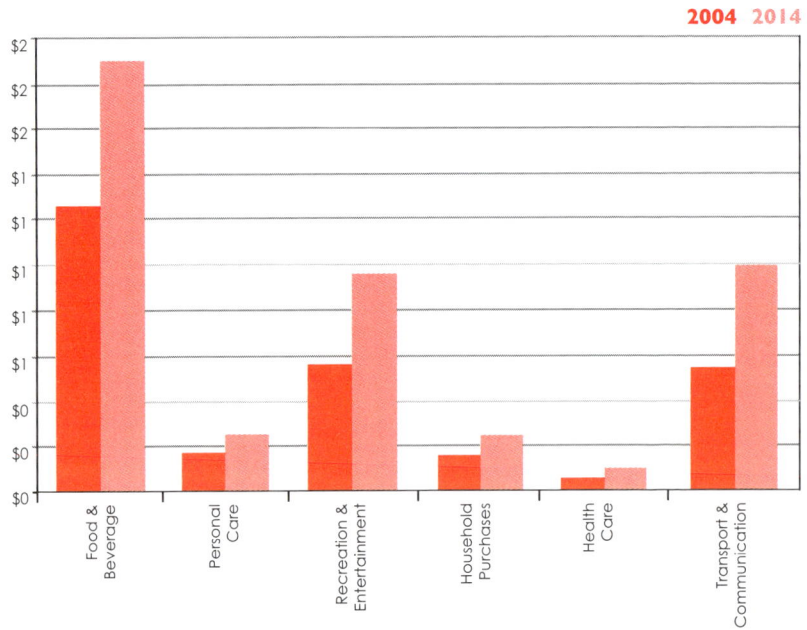

(MasterCard Asia/Pacific, Asian Demographics)

THE PHILIPPINES

SNAPSHOT

population: 80 million
per capita income: $1,000
economic growth: 6.0%
(2004)

Among the major markets in Asia, the Philippines has the youngest population. In 2004, the average age in the Philippines was 26, and will only rise to 30 in 2014. Population growth continues to be high, in spite of some decline in the fertility rate in recent years. From 1970 to 1975, for example, each Filipino woman had on average six children, an astonishingly high level that has more in common with Sub-Saharan Africa than with Asia. The figure is now three, much lower but still high for Asia.

The female literacy rate is high in the Philippines, with close to 95% of all women literate. The secondary school enrolment rate is similarly high, at 85%. These high literacy and education levels, however, have not translated into a high labor force participation rate. In 2003, for example, only half of Filipino women were economically active versus 89% for men. Women are prevented from working due to heavy child bearing responsibilities as most of them marry young and have children almost right away. For most Filipino women, the first 10 to 15 years of married life are consumed with family duties. With the steady decline in fertility, women's labor force participation is expected to rise in the next decade. The number of working women is projected to grow by some 3% a year in the coming decade, versus 2% for men.

The economy, however, suffers from a chronic inability to create enough jobs for the country's young and fast-growing population. As a result, a shocking number, around six million Filipinos (out of a total population of 80 million and a labor force of some 50 million) work overseas. Their remittances of $10 billion a year account for 10% of the economy and are critically important for the poorest one-third of families in meeting their basic needs. In estimating women's total consumption power, these remittances have been taken into account.

Young households have the largest share of Filipino women's total consumption power, estimated at $8 billion, but this figure will grow the most slowly among the groups in the next decade, at only 4%. Middle aged households with children have the second largest share of spending power. It was $9 billion in 2004, and should grow by almost 5% a year to reach $13 billion in 2014. The spending power of both the empty nesters and elderly households are low, estimated at $3 billion and $2 billion respectively in 2004. Their spending power should grow the fastest in the coming decade, at 8% a year for empty nesters and 9% a year for elderly households.

When the spending power is converted to an individual basis, women in young households ranked the lowest, at $1,054 per woman. This is projected to reach $1,225 by 2014. Women in middle aged households, in contrast, had the highest spending power, at $1,600 per woman in 2004, and $1,825 by 2014. These women tend to have large families with many young children so not surprisingly the bulk of their money is spent on taking care of their families. Empty nesters ranked second, with $1,350 per woman, but they will grow the fastest to become the top spender by 2014, with a spending power of $2,160 per woman. Elderly households, on the other hand, will see their spending power of $1,200 per woman increase to $1,460 by 2014.

Table 7.5
THE PHILIPPINES: Women Consumers: Potential Spending Power by Household

US$Billions ($2004)	2004	2014	Av. Annual Growth Rate
Young Households	$17.9	$24.5	3.69%
Middle Aged Households with Children	$8.5	$12.7	4.96%
Empty Nesters (working)	$3.3	$5.9	7.75%
Elderly Households (retired)	$2.2	$4.1	8.53%

(MasterCard Asia/Pacific, Asian Demographics)

Since much of the spending is for basic necessities, discretionary spending power is much lower. For young households, for example, their total spending of $18 billion in 2004 drops to $2 billion in discretionary terms, a mere 11% of the total. The total discretionary spending power for the other groups is even lower. Middle aged households are estimated to have only $800 million of discretionary spending, followed by $300 million for the empty nesters and $200 million for the elderly households. Empty nesters and elderly households will have the highest growth rates, however, estimated at 8% for both groups over the decade to come.

Converting these figures for individuals again shows a different ranking. Middle aged households had the highest discretionary spending, at $152 per woman in 2004, rising to $172 by 2014. The empty nesters came in second, at $123 per woman in 2004, rising to $172 by 2014. They are followed by elderly households, with discretionary spending of $110 per woman in 2004, which is expected to grow to $168 by 2014. Women in young households have the lowest discretionary spending power, estimated at $100 now and $115 per woman in 2014.

At the individual level, Filipino women's discretionary spending power remains low. But these figures are averages. Given that income distribution in the Philippines is among the most unequal in Asia, a small number of women command a disproportionately large share of discretionary spending, whereas the vast majority have even less than the average.

Table 7.6
THE PHILIPPINES: Women Consumers: Total Discretionary Expenditures by Household

US$Billions ($2004)	2004	2014	Av. Annual Growth Rate
Young Households	$1.7	$2.3	3.51%
Middle Aged Households with Children	$0.8	$1.2	4.76%
Empty Nesters (working)	$0.3	$0.6	7.52%
Elderly Households (retired)	$0.2	$0.4	8.28%

(MasterCard Asia/Pacific, Asian Demographics)

The distribution of the discretionary spending by major expenditure items is of a pattern different from other Asian markets. Food and beverage dominate overwhelmingly, and is also expected to grow the fastest. Contrary to the pattern observed in many markets in the region, spending on recreation and entertainment is low—the second lowest, in fact, after health care expenditure, and consistent with the Philippines' low numbers in outbound travel (for personal holidays as opposed to seeking work overseas). Personal care expenditure is the second highest, followed by spending on household appliances, then transportation and communication. But all these items are small as shares of total discretionary spending, making up less than 40% of the total.

Chart 7.3
THE PHILIPPINES: Women Consumers: Key Discretionary Expenditures by Household Segment

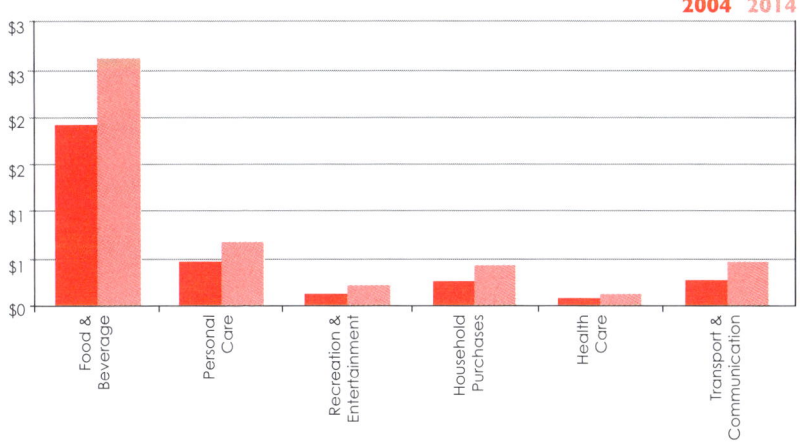

(MasterCard Asia/Pacific, Asian Demographics)

THAILAND

> **SNAPSHOT**
>
> population: 63 million
> per capita income: $3,000
> economic growth: 6.1%
> (2004)

The average Thai is aged 32, and the figure is expected to rise to 40 in 10 years' time. Thus Thailand is a "middle-aged" country, not quite as old as Japan, Korea, Australia and China, but older than India, Malaysia and the Philippines. The government's successful family planning programs in the 1970s and 1980s are largely responsible for these figures. The fertility rate of the average Thai woman, for example, was high at five in the 1970s but today is 1.9, just below replacement level.

Thai women are well educated. Female literacy is virtually 100% in urban areas, and around 90% in rural areas. All women under the age of 40 are basically literate. Women's secondary enrolment rate is an impressive 82%. Indeed, in tertiary education, women outperform men. Thai women scored the highest in the objective score of the MasterIndex of Women's Advancement in 2004. The score of 107.4 means that for every 100 Thai men with tertiary education in the labor force, there were 107.4 Thai women with a similar level of education and an even higher labor force participation rate. These figures are a truly stunning achievement.

The tourism industry, which makes up 10% of the economy, is a major source of jobs, benefiting retailers and small business operators. Many of these small business proprietors are women. For the young and better educated, careers opportunities can be found in the international hotel chains, travel agencies, airlines and so on.

One important feature of Thai women is that, like their Malaysian counterparts, they are assertive and self-confident consumers. This fact is reflected in their subjective score of MasterIndex of Woman's Advancement, an impressive 77.3, meaning for every 100 Thai men who believed that they are in managerial positions and earn above average income, 77.3 Thai women believed the same.

As shown in Table 7.7, women in young households have the highest spending among the four household groups, followed by middle aged households, then empty nesters and lastly the elderly households. The same ranking will hold by 2014. In growth rates, however, the order is reversed. Spending power will grow the fastest among elderly households, estimated at 15% a year in the next decade, followed by empty nesters at 13%. In contrast, the growth rate is 6% and 3% respectively for middle aged households and young households.

On an individual basis, the picture also looks different. Women in middle aged households had the highest spending power at $1,974 per woman in 2004, rising to $2,865 by 2014. The empty nesters ranked second, with $1,500 per woman in 2004, and $2,300 by 2014. The elderly households were in third place, with about $1,500 in 2004, rising to $2,260 by 2014. Women in the young households had the lowest spending individually; $1,420 in 2004 and $2,110 by 2014.

Table 7.7
THAILAND: Women Consumers: Potential Spending Power by Household

US$Billions ($2004)	2004	2014	Av. Annual Growth Rate
Young Households	$18.4	$24.2	3.15%
Middle Aged Households with Children	$10.3	$16.2	5.74%
Empty Nesters (working)	$6.5	$14.9	12.77%
Elderly Households (retired)	$3.6	$8.9	14.50%

(MasterCard Asia/Pacific, Asian Demographics)

In discretionary spending, the pattern is identical to that of total spending power of the four households. Young households have the biggest share, followed by middle aged households, then the empty nesters, with elderly households coming in last. But their respective growth rates are in a reversed order in the next decade—the elderly households segment will grow by 15% per year, the empty nesters at 13%, the middle aged households 6%, and the young households 3%.

The picture again looks completely different when the spending power is evaluated on an individual basis. Women in the middle aged households had the highest discretionary spending, at $192 per woman. Elderly households ranked second. with $165 per woman. The empty nesters were third, with $138 per woman, and young households in last place, with $139 per woman.

By 2014, however, empty nesters will be number one, with $321 per woman in discretionary spending. Women in middle aged households will drop to second place, with $282 per woman. Elderly households will hold third place, with $229 per woman, and the young households, again, in the last place, with $209 per woman. These estimates of individual discretionary spending are only just above those for the Philippines. The big difference is that income distribution is more equal in Thailand than it is in the Philippines. In Thailand there are more women consumers, each with a moderate amount of discretionary spending, than there are in the Philippines.

Table 7.8
THAILAND: Women Consumers: Total Discretionary Expenditures by Household

US$Billions ($2004)	2004	2014	Av. Annual Growth Rate
Young Households	$1.8	$2.4	3.18%
Middle Aged Households with Children	$1.0	$1.6	5.77%
Empty Nesters (working)	$0.6	$1.5	12.82%
Elderly Households (retired)	$0.4	$0.9	14.56%

(MasterCard Asia/Pacific, Asian Demographics)

Food and beverage are the most important expenditure items, and will remain so for the next decade. But communication and transportation are the fastest growing, reflecting a rise in car ownership. This is followed by recreation and entertainment, also fast growing expenditure items. In comparison, expenditures on personal care and household appliances are small, and are not expected to be fast growing.

Chart 7.4
THAILAND: Women Consumers: Key Discretionary Expenditures by Household Segment

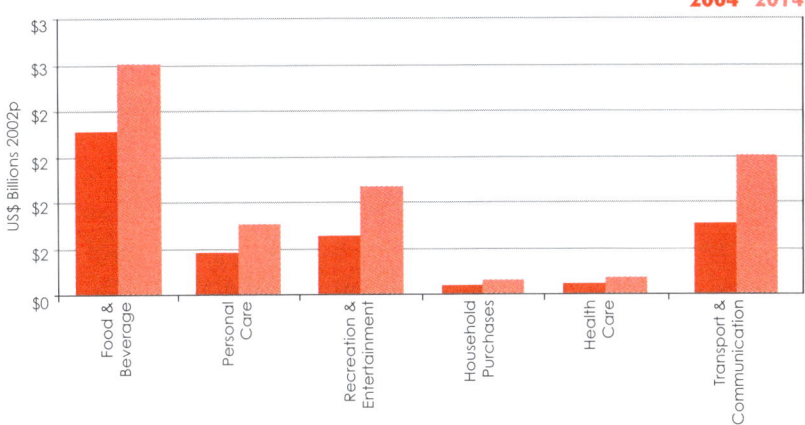

(MasterCard Asia/Pacific, Asian Demographics)

CONCLUSION: WHAT DO WOMEN WANT? 8

Women consumers are fast becoming an important market in Asia. Young women, especially the young singles, are urban, trendy and pioneering fast-moving lifestyles. Elderly women consumers, on the other hand, are venturing into uncharted territory as they live longer, healthier and more active lives.

The rise of women consumers in Asia has much to do with the changing role of women as producers in society. The trends are unmistakable. Women are becoming better educated and more active in the workforce. More of them are pursuing professional careers, and postponing marriage and children. And when they do settle down to have a family, most opt for one or two children at most. For elderly women, especially those in affluent Asia, many will stay active into their 70s and 80s in the coming decade, seeking new experiences and ventures. Their rising discretionary spending power will be a key driver of Asian consumer markets, and no business can afford to ignore them.

Women's rising income in Asia has ushered in new patterns of consumption. With more women working, for example, a simple activity like shopping has been transformed. Time has become a scarce resource for working women, and when they shop for basic necessities they want the experience to be fast, convenient and with minimum fuss; hence the rapid and successful emergence of supermarkets and hypermarkets in Asian cities.

Rising income also means a shift from buying basic necessities to discretionary spending. As we have seen in the previous chapters, women consumers in Asia are spending more on dining out, personal travel, visiting health spas, and other recreational and leisure activities. Working women are more likely to need a car as well as have the means to buy one. They want their own computers and accessories at home. They are inclined to spend more on pampering themselves and are more likely to have a gym membership close to the office so they can exercise during lunch hours.

For the elderly women, discretionary spending is more likely to center on social activities with close friends and relatives. Unlike younger consumers, they are in the market to buy new and enjoyable experiences, not new gadgets. Even when it comes to shopping, elderly women's preference is unlikely to be large glittering malls with loud pounding music. They prefer quieter and more intimate settings where they can spend enjoyable hours with friends. For those elderly women who can afford it, they will enthusiastically pursue new hobbies and studies, usually with friends. In Japan, for example, private schools flourish offering classes ranging from calligraphy to flower arrangement, computers, traditional arts and crafts, yoga and taichi, and so forth. Continuing education is in high demand. And it is precisely this kind of discretionary spending that is having the most direct and powerful impact on businesses.

In the six countries included in affluent Asia, the total discretionary spending power of women consumers is estimated at $282 billion. It is projected to grow only modestly at a rate of 2% to reach $335 billion by 2014.

Table 8.1
Discretionary Spending by Women in Affluent Asia

$ billion	2004	2014
Australia	22	27
Hong Kong	6	9
Japan	203	228
Korea	30	44
Singapore	3	4
Taiwan	19	23
Total	283	335
Average annual rate of growth		1.7%

(MasterCard Asia/Pacific)

In emerging Asia, the average annual growth is expected to be higher at 6%. For the five countries included, the total discretionary spending power of their women consumers in 2004 was estimated at $103 billion, just over one-third that of affluent Asia. By 2014, however, their discretionary spending power is projected to rise to $183 billion, or about half that of affluent Asia.

Table 8.2
Discretionary Spending by Women in Emerging Asia

$ billion	2004	2014
China	66	120
India	27	47
Malaysia	3	5
Philippines	3	5
Thailand	4	6
Total	103	183
Average annual rate of growth		5.9%

(MasterCard Asia/Pacific)

DISCRETIONARY SPENDING BY WOMEN IN YOUNG HOUSEHOLDS

Within this market, young singles and young marrieds with no children are the most avid spenders when it comes to discretionary consumption. The young marrieds with a child under 10, on the other hand, tend to be preoccupied with bringing up the child, who dictates spending priorities.

Asian women in the young singles and young married stages are well known for being fashion conscious. Young Japanese women, for example, spend twice as much as their American counterparts on branded luxury goods. Japan alone accounts for 40% of global luxury goods sales, with China being the fastest-growing market for high-end designer products.[1] And it is not surprising that this generation of young women is sometimes referred to as the "me" generation. They are also a wired generation, blurring the boundary between gadgets and fashion. Increasingly, electronic gadgets need to compete on both function and style.

Of the six countries included in affluent Asia, about 40 million women are in young households. Because of the ageing population, their number will shrink slightly to 36 million by 2014, a decline of 1% a year. The size of the young singles segment will remain almost unchanged over the next decade as more young women are opting for a singles lifestyle. The discretionary spending of this group will grow only marginally from $103 billion in 2004 to $106 billion in 2014.

Table 8.3

Discretionary Spending by Women in Young Households Segment in Affluent Asia

	2004		2014	
	Population (million)	Spending ($ billion)	Population (million)	Spending ($ billion)
Hong Kong	1.4	2	1.2	2
Australia	3.4	9	3.4	10
Japan	20.7	69	17.9	68
Korea	9.5	14	8.4	16
Singapore	0.58	1	0.62	1
Taiwan	4.5	8	4.2	9
Total	39.9	103	35.7	106
Average annual rate of growth			-1.2%	+0.3%

(MasterCard Asia/Pacific)

The populations are younger in emerging Asia, with China being the sole exception. The rapid decline of women in young households in China overwhelms the growing trend in the other countries. In 2004, there were 241 million women in this group in China. By 2014, the figure will be down to about 148 million. So the overall size of the group in all five countries will be declining by about 1% a year in the next decade, from 491 million to 433 million. In spite of their declining numbers, the discretionary spending power of these women will be increasing, reflecting rising incomes. Women in this group commanded some $54 billion of discretionary spending power in 2004. It will rise to $82 billion by 2014, an increase of 4% a year.

Table 8.4
Discretionary Spending by Women in Young Households Segment in Emerging Asia

	2004		2014	
	Population (million)	Spending ($ billion)	Population (million)	Spending ($ billion)
China	241.0	30	147.7	45
India	215.1	18	247.9	30
Malaysia	5.3	2	6.2	2
Philippines	16.9	2	19.9	3
Thailand	12.9	2	11.5	2
Total	491.2	54	433.2	82
Average annual rate of growth			-1%	+4%

(MasterCard Asia/Pacific)

DISCRETIONARY SPENDING BY WOMEN IN MIDDLE AGED WITH CHILDREN HOUSEHOLDS

Women in this group are concerned chiefly with raising children and caring for their families. Because of declining fertility in both affluent and emerging Asia, the overall size of this group is also relatively small, when compared with young households and elderly households. In discretionary spending, about 15 million women in this group in affluent Asia spent $16 billion in 2004. By 2014, it is expected that about 16 million women in this group will spend $56 billion.

Table 8.5
Discretionary Spending by Women in Middle Aged Households Segment in Affluent Asia

	2004		2014	
	Population (million)	Spending ($ billion)	Population (million)	Spending ($ billion)
Hong Kong	0.65	2	0.67	2
Australia	1.3	4	1.6	5
Japan	7.7	31	8.0	34
Korea	3.2	6	3.8	9
Singapore	0.26	1	0.28	1
Taiwan	1.5	4	1.8	5
Total	14.6	48	16.1	56
Average annual rate of growth			+1.0%	+1.6%

(MasterCard Asia/Pacific)

In emerging Asia, 213 million women in this group had $27 billion in discretionary spending in 2004. This figure is low on a per woman basis—$127. By 2014, the 236 million women in this group are expected to have $46 billion in discretionary spending—$195 per woman, an increase of 6% a year.

Table 8.6
Discretionary Spending by Women in Middle Aged Households Segment in Emerging Asia

	2004		2014	
	Population (million)	Spending ($ billion)	Population (million)	Spending ($ billion)
China	15.5	19	118.1	31
India	84.9	6	102.5	11
Malaysia	1.9	1	2.5	1
Philippines	5.2	1	6.9	1
Thailand	5.2	1	5.6	2
Total	212.7	28	235.6	46
Average annual rate of growth			+1%	+6%

(MasterCard Asia/Pacific)

DISCRETIONARY SPENDING BY WOMEN IN ELDERLY HOUSEHOLDS

The number of women in elderly households, in both affluent and emerging Asia, is the fastest growing, reflecting the general ageing trend in the region. In 2004, some 42 million women in this group were in affluent Asia, and by 2014, this group should grow to over 50 million women.

In affluent Asia, more women in this group will be living healthier and active lives. Many will outlive their spouses. Increasingly, companionship with friends is the key social bond for these women. This form of bonding among elderly single women will have far-reaching implications on their priorities and preferences as consumers. Businesses must focus on this trend if they wish to be successful in attracting the elderly, and increasingly single, women as customers. Surprisingly, it is also an area much ignored in market research, but will become clearly important in coming years. Elderly women consumers in affluent Asia have collectively $131 billion of discretionary spending power and by 2014 will have $172 billion, or a significant sum of $3,400 per woman.

Table 8.7

Discretionary Spending by Women in Empty Nesters and Elderly Households Segment in Affluent Asia

	2004		2014	
	Population (million)	Spending ($ billion)	Population (million)	Spending ($ billion)
Hong Kong	1.0	2	1.6	4
Australia	2.9	9	3.5	11
Japan	28.1	103	31.7	126
Korea	6.5	10	8.9	19
Singapore	0.5	1	0.7	2
Taiwan	2.9	6	3.9	10
Total	41.9	131	50.3	172
Average annual rate of growth			+2%	+3%

(MasterCard Asia/Pacific)

In emerging Asia, there are 218 million women in elderly households. This figure is expected to grow by 4% a year, and, by 2014, it will reach 330 million. Not surprisingly, their discretionary spending power is much lower than their counterparts in affluent Asia. In 2004, their collective discretionary spending was $23 billion. By 2014, their discretionary spending is projected to grow 9% a year to about $55 billion, or $167 per woman.

Table 8.8
Discretionary Spending by Women in Empty Nesters and Elderly Households Segment in Emerging Asia

	2004		2014	
	Population (million)	Spending ($ billion)	Population (million)	Spending ($ billion)
China	156.4	18	238.0	44
India	49.1	3	73.3	6
Malaysia	1.3	1	2.1	1
Philippines	4.2	1	6.2	1
Thailand	6.7	1	10.4	2
Total	217.7	24	330.0	54
Average annual rate of growth			+4.2%	+%

(MasterCard Asia/Pacific)

THE RISING TREND OF WOMEN TRAVELERS

Regardless of their specific stages and whether they live in affluent or emerging Asia, a common thread in Asia is the dramatic increase of women taking to travel as part of their lifestyle. To understand how much women consumers are willing to spend on travel, it is worth taking a deeper look. The number of women travelers in the region is impressive. The ratio of male to female travelers has been shifting in favor of females—from around 90:10 (males to females) 30 years ago, to around 60:40 today. Korean visitor arrivals illustrate this trend. In 1975, the ratio was 89:11 (males to females). Twenty-five years later it had shifted to 58:42.

Chart 8.1
Gender Mix of Arrivals, Korea*

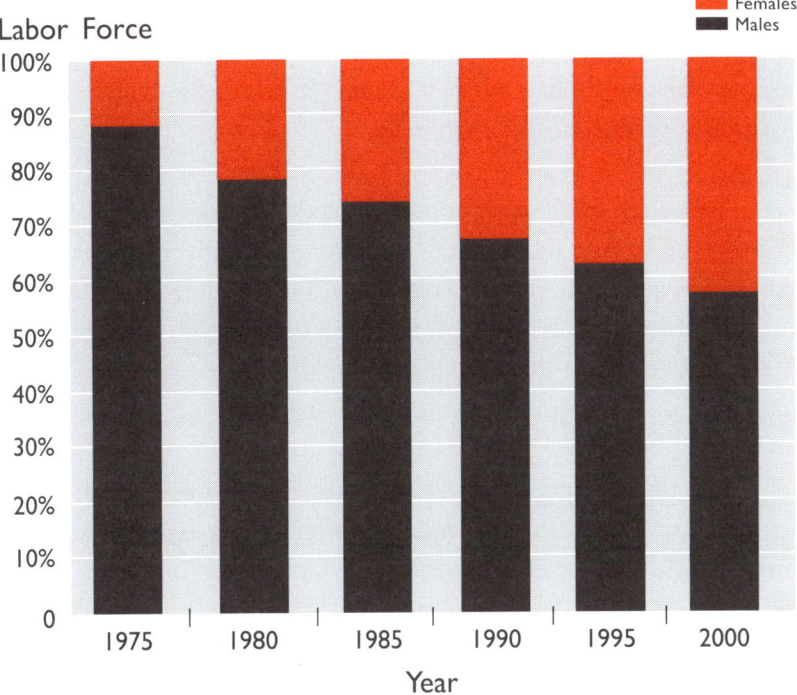

(Korea National Tourism Organization, 2002. *Figures for 2002 are the same as for 2000.)

Thus, the number of women visitors to Asia has been increasing as well as women's share of the travel market. If we take the 60:40 ratio, we can assume that around 64 million of the 160 million individuals who traveled in Asia were women.

And women's share has the potential to rise even more. Ratios in the developed travel markets of the USA and Europe are closer to 50:50, and Asia is likely to follow this trend. The Japanese market, arguably the most developed in the region, may point the way. The most recent figures show a ratio of 55:45 (males to females). Singapore's ratio is 56:44. At present the only market group that achieves this magic balance is Japanese honeymooners, who are guaranteed to have a 50:50 ratio! In fact, more women will likely travel than men in the long term. The Australian short-term holiday departures (overseas holidays less than 12 months long) are already dominated by women. In 2000, the ratio was 46:54 for male versus female. Thailand and New Zealand consistently receive more Australian female visitors than male.

Although 60:40 does appear to be the average male to female visitor ratio in Asia today, there are wide gender divergences within visitor arrivals from various countries. In Singapore, for example, the ratio for China arrivals is almost 50:50, while for Indian arrivals, it is still two-thirds men. Thailand, on the other hand, gets more male visitors (excepting Australian tourists).

To understand these trends, one must know more about women travelers. The biannual MasterCard's Asian Lifestyles Survey yields some valuable insights. The survey monitors travel attitudes and trends among male and female travelers in 13 countries in Asia. The male to female ratio of those surveyed is indeed 60:40 according to the survey. Travel has become a way of life for women in Asia. Approximately three quarters of them consider travel important for their lifestyles, and 37% reported that they have taken at least one international flight for personal purposes in the past 12 months.

Another survey conducted by the Japan Association of Travel Agents (JATA) in 2003 confirms this trend for the Japanese market. But it also reveals that internet usage is age-related. It is surprising that more Japanese women in their 30s and 40s report that they make travel decisions based on the internet, than women in their 20s. The results of this survey also suggest that women in their 50s and 60s are becoming tech savvy, with those in their 60s reporting high usage. Catering to these tech-savvy women are the growing numbers of women-specific travel websites. Journeywoman, for example, is a premier travel resource for women, very interactive and chatty, with an emphasis on sharing experiences, tips and information. Women have also organized online travel clubs, which cater exclusively to group tours for women. General sites for Asian women have begun to feature travel information, such the Malaysian site www.i-asianwomen.com. In addition, there is a growing niche in travel books for women, such as China for Women: Travel and Culture, and The Smart Woman's Guide to Business Travel.

Women are great travel planners too. Travel consultant Marybeth Bond reports that for family travel in the USA, 70% of travel decisions are made by women.[2] The CEO of a large California travel agency confirmed that 70% to 75% of the decision-makers they deal with are women. Checks with travel agents in Singapore appear to confirm this figure. If this 70% figure holds, then the implications for the travel industry are profound.

One dimension of women travelers is utterly unique to Asia. They are dedicated shoppers. According to the MasterCard's Asian Lifestyles Survey, shopping ranks a clear first as a preferred destination activity for women. Major Asian cities such as Seoul, Hong Kong, Bangkok and Singapore vie for the tourist shopping dollar, and this means primarily appealing to women shoppers. This emphasis on shopping is corroborated by a recent Japan Tourism Marketing survey, which shows shopping as the preferred activity of 79% female travelers. The next closest chosen activities were visiting natural and scenic attractions (61%); rest and relaxation (48%); gourmet cuisine sampling (42%) and visiting historic and cultural attractions (37%).

Asian women are not only dedicated shoppers, but also well-prepared. Japanese women traveling to shop often make elaborate preparations before departure. First, they research their favorite brand manufacturers by ordering product catalogues or brochures and consulting the latest fashion magazines. Next they visit shops in Japan to view the products hands-on, and check out the prices for comparison later. Finally, they compile a list of their selected items, which contains product information—including photographs, domestic prices and addresses of the shops in their destinations that carry the items. Well prepared indeed.

Table 8.9
Ranking of Reasons for Travel

	MEN	WOMEN
1	beach resorts	shopping/entertainment
2	culture/historic	culture/historic
3	shopping/entertainment	beach resorts
4	nature/adventure	nature/adventure
5	family resorts	family resorts

(MasterCard Asia/Pacific)

Women travelers are universally more concerned than men on some key issues. The most important is, not surprisingly, safety. Men and women travelers share concerns about terrorism, aircraft reliability and health issues such as SARS and bird flu. But women focus on physical safety. They like to know if the hotel they book is safe and in a good neighborhood. Within the hotel they like to know if the corridors are well-lit, if lifts are secure, and if doors have double locks. They are more likely to check a travel agency's reputation, particularly how it caters to female travelers. Next is psychological safety—including how comfortable they are with the culture, religion and general surroundings of the destination. Safety issues, physical and psychological, may well be a major reason for the popularity of Hawaii as a holiday destination for Japanese. According to a 2001 survey by the Japanese newspaper *Mainichi Shimbun*, Hawaii ranked as the safest destination for Japanese tourists, far ahead of Australia, Switzerland, the UK, Canada and Singapore.

For women travelers, word of mouth rates number one, with the internet and travel agents tying for second place as sources of information. Men, on the other hand, appear to be more likely to use the internet as their first planning source. Not that women are less tech savvy. It might be that as women place a high priority on safety, they therefore place more value on personal recommendations.

Table 8.10
Planning for Travel: Top Five Travel Sources (most important first)

	MEN	WOMEN
1	internet	word of mouth
2	word of mouth	internet or travel agent (tie)
3	travel agent	guide books
4	guide books	newspapers
5	newspapers	

(MasterCard Asia/Pacific)

MasterCard's Asian Lifestyles Survey confirms that men and women have different preferences for travel in Asia. In fact, they have diametrically opposite picks of their top three countries in Asia: China, Thailand and Singapore for women; and Singapore, Thailand and China for men. This tantalizing piece of information shows that gender preferences must figure more prominently in research on travelers in the Asia.

Table 8.11

Preferred Destinations – Personal Travel: Top Six Destinations (first is most preferred)

	MEN	WOMEN
1	Singapore	China
2	Thailand	Thailand
3	China	Singapore
4	Malaysia	Hong Kong
5	Australia	Australia/Malaysia (tie)

(MasterCard Asia/Pacific)

To better understand women travelers in Asia, it helps to know more about the context within which they have emerged in recent decades. One surprise is a study in Japan, for example, that recently noted that women in their 60s are more active at their destinations than women in their 20s. Japanese senior travelers posted the highest increase of any age group. They are also growing fast as an age group. By 2025, about one third of the Japanese population will be 65 or older.[3] The "mature" market clearly is of growing importance when it comes to women travelers, not only in Japan, but across the region as well.

As illustrated in Chart 8.2, more women traveled in 2002 than in 1997, the only exception being those in the 20 to 29 years old and the 40 to 49 years old brackets. More women over 50 years old have started traveling in recent years, and the rate of increase is particularly striking among women over 60 years old.

Chart 8.2
Japanese Women Travelers
Labour Force

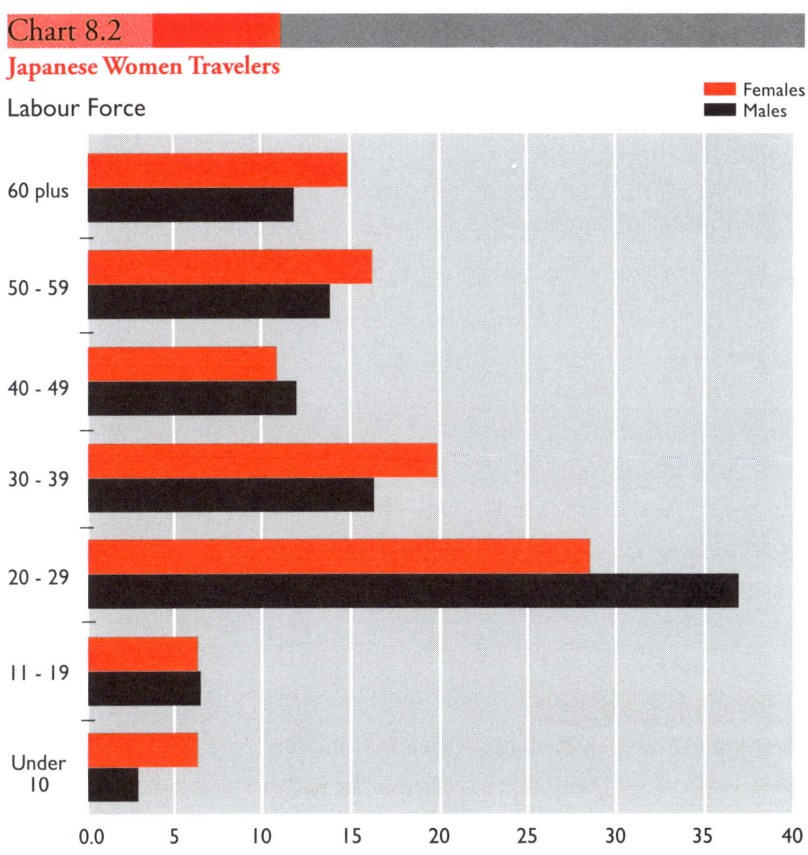

(Japan Travel Blue Book 2003/04)

Another important market about which far too little is known is pre-teenage girls. An article in the latest issue of Japan Travel Blue Book reveals several unanticipated facts about this market. For one thing, educational tours are marketing to ever-younger children. *Nicola*, a Japanese children's magazine, teamed up with Geos Study Tours to organize study trips to Australia for children aged 10 to14. *Nicola* reports the children themselves call to sign up, responding to ads in *Nicola*. And their most popular activity is, surprise, shopping. According to Geos Study Tours, the greatest interest that female children had was the opportunity to travel with one of the fashion models featured regularly in *Nicola* who enjoys the status of a teen idol among her adoring young fans. When the model purchased an item during the tour every child bought the same one of the same color. Japanese women shoppers are honing their skills at ever earlier ages.

Breakdowns of age group statistics by gender can offer new insights into the rapidly changing face of internet travel options. According to a recent JATA survey, while men in their 20s are most likely to use the internet for travel research and planning, women in their 30s, in contrast, are the most avid internet users for the same purposes. And, surprisingly, one third of senior women travelers, those in their 60s and above, reported that they use the internet for travel planning (and nearly half of all senior men travelers use the internet as well).

Table 8.12

**Decision to Travel on the Basis of Web Information
(percentage of age group that use internet for decision-making)**

AGE GROUP	MEN (%)	WOMEN (%)
20s	70	52
30s	56	62
40s	62	59
50s	50	31
60s	46	35
Total	53	47

(JATA Survey)

Gender issues are often ignored in travel analyses. A closer look allows two conclusions. First, women's relative share of visitor arrivals in Asia has been climbing, from around 90:10 (males to females) 25 years ago, to the present 60:40 and will continue to move in favor of women, closer to a developed market ratio of one to one. And similar trends are clear in the most developed markets of Asia, including Japan, Singapore and Korea. In fact, if one takes passport applications as an intention to travel abroad, then there are actually more women than men applying for passports in Japan—52% for females versus 48% for males. Not only are more women traveling. They tend to remain active travelers much longer in their lives, especially as they remain healthier longer. More Japanese women than men apply for passports in their 70s and 80s.

Compared with Western women travelers, Asian women travelers will think nothing of hopping on a plane for a shopping weekend. Pampering at spas is preferred to rough adventure trips. And Asian women are more inclined to factor families into holiday travel. In the West, peer group travel is the norm for single women (joining tours, traveling with friends or colleagues). In Asia, mothers and daughters are a common travel unit. What is the bottom line on women's spending on shopping when they travel? Estimates made for four key tourist destination cities, Bangkok, Hong Kong, Seoul and Singapore, show that by 2011 about $20 billion a year will be spent by tourists on shopping in these cities.[4] Assuming conservatively that women travelers spend twice as much as men on shopping, and assuming that by 2011 the ratio between men and women travelers will be 50:50, it means women travelers will command some $13 billion of spending power in these four cities alone. For anyone who wants to capture this huge emerging consumer market, it is time to try to understand properly who they are, what they want and how they want what they want. Watch the women.

CONCLUSION

With an estimated $516 billion of discretionary spending power under their command by 2014—$335 billion in affluent Asia and $181 billion in emerging Asia—women consumers in Asia are unquestionably a power to be reckoned with. Capturing this fantastic business potential, however, requires an indepth understanding of women's rapidly evolving lifestyles in Asia, especially in terms of their specific lifecycle stages. This new frontier of market research is indispensable to any businesses that want to win the hearts and wallets of Asia's women consumers.

FOOTNOTES

Chapter 1
1. Landes, D. 1999. *The Wealth and Poverty of Nations*. New York: W.W. Norton & Co.
2. Humana, C. 1992. World Human Rights Guide. New York: Oxford University Press.
3. Easterlin, R. 1998. Growth Triumphant. Ann Arbor: University of Michigan Press.
4. See Dollar, D. and R. Gatti, 1999. "Gender Inequality, Income and Growth: Are Good Times Good for Women?" World Bank; and Easterly, W. 2002. The Elusive Quest for Growth. Cambridge: MIT Press.
5. India, Bangladesh, Pakistan, Nepal and Sri Lanka.
6. It is estimated some 30 million Chinese died from the ensuing famine because the crops were neglected.

Chapter 2
1. The countries included are: Japan, Korea, China, Taiwan, Hong Kong SAR, Singapore, Thailand, Malaysia, Indonesia, the Philippines, India and Australia.

Chapter 3
1. Fertility rate (or more accurately "total fertility rate") refers to the number of children a woman has in her lifetime.
2. *Howls of the Loser Dogs*, by Junko Sakai.
3. Hakuhodo Institute of Life and Living Study.
4. Hakuhodo Institute of Life and Living Study.
5. John McCreery, Japanese Consumer Behavior: From Worker Bees to Wary Shoppers.
6. *The Chrysanthemum and the Sword*. 1946.
7. All forecasts are made in constant 2004 $.
8. Meaning on average there are 1.29 children in each woman's reproductive cycle; which is below the replacement rate of 2.0.
9. Korea National Statistical Office.

Chapter 5
1. According to a survey conducted by Monash University, some 69% of women believe they should stay home as long as they have children who are still going to school to look after.
2. Australian Bureau of Statistics, Social Trends, 2004.

Chapter 6
1 Survey by China Central Television Station and the China National Statistics Bureau, 2000.
2 Conducted by horizonkey.com.
3 Prof. Tom Shaosu, Zhejiang University, china.org.cn, January 2, 2003.

Chapter 8
1 CLSA Emerging Markets Research, Buckle, Karen, 2005
2 www.marybethbond.com
3 Japan National Tourist Organization.
4 See Benefiting from the Synergy Between Travel and Retail. MasterCard Asia/Pacific Insights Series, 2Q, 2004.

INDEX

386 generation 65

A

A-A couple 111, 112
accumulated privately held assets 51
affluent and emerging Asia 142, 144
affluent Asia 43, 67, 71, 87, 137, 139, 141, 143, 144, 145, 156
affluent households 118
ageing pattern 89
ageing trend 58, 77, 80, 85, 89, 112, 144
ageing population 44, 45, 72, 90, 141
airlines 132
atomization of the traditional household 64
attitude and behavior of women consumers 11
average annual income 43, 118
average household income 51
average life expectancy 81

B

baby boomers 12, 21, 65, 91, 95
Beijing 104, 107, 111
Benedict, Ruth 52
Bond, Marybeth 149
bonds and stocks 110
branded luxury goods 140

C

Canada 151
car ownership 126, 134
career opportunities 12, 123
centenarians 24
changing lifestyles 25, 29
child-rearing 13, 19, 60
China for Women: Travel and Culture 149
China's geopolitical clout 102
Chinese Cultural Revolution 12
communication and transportation 134
computers and accessories 138
Confucian value system 61
consumer credit and loans 110
consumer force 69,
consumer market 1, 6, 7, 11, 13, 17, 24, 32, 41, 48, 52, 53, 66, 72, 91, 95, 96, 97, 100, 102, 138, 155
consumer preferences 8
consumption dynamics 64
consumption revolution 7, 10
costs of education 59
credit 109, 110
cyberspace 65

D

decline in population growth 108
declining birth rate 59
delay in motherhood 90

delayed marriage 110
demographic and economic trends, lifestyle trends 65, 88, 95, 100
demographic shift 81, 83
demographic shock 102, 103
demographic trends 23, 24, 45
demographics xi, 20, 88
DINK (double income, no kids) 111
discretionary consumption 140
discretionary expenditure 55, 56, 67, 68, 76, 79, 80, 84, 85, 99, 100, 115, 116, 120, 121, 122, 125, 126, 132-5
discretionary spenders 81
discretionary spending power 54, 55, 79, 84, 99, 114, 121, 129, 130, 138, 139, 142, 145, 156
disparity between the sexes 92
disposable income 13, 14, 17-19, 20, 32, 110, 121
domestic consumption 6, 7
dynamic market segment 126

E

earning power 92, 95, 108
economic development and income levels 41
economic structural shift 81
education 1, 3-6, 12, 18, 19, 49, 50, 52, 59, 60, 62, 63, 65, 83, 88, 93, 102, 106, 108, 109, 118, 123, 127, 132, 139, 153
educational and workforce participation 5
educational tours 153
elderly household 20, 23, 25-7, 29, 30, 32, 34-9, 40, 53-6, 66-8, 75-9, 83, 84, 98, 99, 113-5, 120, 121, 124, 125, 128, 129, 130, 132-4, 143-6
elderly retired households 74, 75, 78, 81, 83
elderly single women 48, 144

elderly women 20, 23, 24, 26, 27, 30, 39, 41, 45, 47, 50, 53, 54, 80, 85, 137, 138, 145
emerging consumer market 155
emerging countries 43
employment opportunities 109, 123
empty nesters 18, 19, 20, 21, 23, 25-7, 29, 30, 32, 34-7, 39, 40, 47, 50, 53-5, 66-8, 73-9, 81, 83, 84, 90, 97-9, 105, 112-5, 119, 120, 121, 124, 125, 128, 129, 130, 132-4, 145, 146
entertainment and recreation 77
Equal Employment Opportunity Law 48
evolving lifestyles 85, 156
Ewha Women's University 60
expenditure items 130, 134

F

families 13, 18, 19, 23, 102, 103, 111, 119, 123, 128, 142, 155
female literacy 127, 132
female unemployment rate 2, 3
fertility rate 44, 103, 123, 127, 131
  decline in fertility 103, 127
  declining fertility 44, 46, 142
  declining fertility rate 44
F-Generation 111, 112
finance, real estate and business services 77
financial and personal services 123
financial hub 78
food and beverage 55, 56, 79, 80, 100, 115, 122, 125, 130, 134

G

gender preferences 151
Generation X 13, 14
Generation Y 13, 14
generational perspectives 66
Geos Study Tours 153
Gray Market 21

Great Leap Forward 101
Guangdong Province 111
Guangzhou 111

H
Hawaii 151
health and fitness-related services 110
health care 44, 68, 79, 84, 99, 100, 130
health sciences and biomedical production 82
hippy culture 111
holiday travel 155
hospitality services 123
household appliances 130, 134
household purchases 56, 68, 79, 84
Howl of the Loser Dogs 46

I
immigrants 45
income distribution 130, 134
information technology 65
infrastructure development 108
inheritance 51, 95
intergenerational holidays 14
international hotel chains 132
internet 13, 110, 148, 151, 154
internet travel options 154
internet usage 148
investment finance 78
Italy and Sweden 45

J
Japan Association of Travel Agents (JATA) 148
Japan Tourism Marketing survey 149
Japan Travel Blue Book 153
Japanese honeymooners 147
Japanese Office Ladies 13, 14
job creation 78
job market 76, 124
Journeywoman 148
junior colleges 147

K
knowledge intensive 27, 94
knowledge intensive economy 27
knowledge-intensive manufacturing 82
knowledge workers 107
Koizumi, Junichiro 9

L
labor force participation 2-4, 6, 55, 88, 102, 118, 119, 123, 127, 132
labor force participation rate 50, 123, 127, 132
labor intensive manufacturing 106
Landes, David, *The Wealth and Poverty of Nations* 1
leisure-related pursuits 76
Li, Yinhe 111
lifestyle 13, 20, 25, 29, 32, 48, 50-3, 57, 59, 64, 65, 76, 80, 81, 85, 99, 100, 111, 112, 114, 115, 137, 141, 146, 149, 151, 156
lifestyle changes 57
lifestyle orientation 121
lifestyle trends 18, 65, 100
literacy 127, 132
"loser dogs" 46, 49

M
M Curve 49
Mainichi Shimbun 151
male-to-female birth ratio 104
managerial position 3, 4, 126, 132
managing family finances 109
manufacturing 61, 62, 63, 77, 81, 82, 91, 93, 96, 106, 107, 123
market research 145, 156
market sizes and rates of population growth 41
me generation 13, 14
middle aged 18, 19, 23, 25-7, 29, 30, 32, 34, 35, 37, 39, 40, 53-5, 66, 67, 74-6, 78, 79, 81, 83, 84, 98,

99, 104, 106, 110, 113-5, 119, 120, 121, 124, 125, 128, 129, 130, 132-4, 142-4
middle aged household 23, 25, 26, 29, 30, 32, 34, 35, 37, 39, 40, 53-5, 66, 67, 74-6, 78, 79, 81, 83, 84, 98, 99, 104, 106, 110, 113-5, 119, 120, 121, 124, 125, 128, 129, 130, 132-4, 142-4
middle aged married 18, 19, 26, 83, 113, 114
middle aged with children households 34, 119, 120, 144
middle aged women with children 81
middle income 35
Ministry of Gender Equality 61
mobile technology connectivity 94
mortgage-free 20

N
National People's Congress 106
new consumer market 32
New Old People's Movement 51
new urban lifestyles 112
New Zealand 148
N-generation (the Net generation) 65
Nicola (magazine) 153, 154

O
"old" old age 51, 53
old single women households 66
old singles 51, 66, 91, 112, 113
older women 33, 34, 55, 58, 97, 99, 100, 106, 108
older working age empty nesters 90
one-child policy 103, 104, 110, 112
online travel clubs 149

P
pace of change 11
part-time workers 48, 92
passport applications 155

patterns of consumption 138
peer group activities 99
peer group travel 155
pensions 95
personal care 55, 68, 79, 84, 115, 130, 134
personal travel 76, 115, 122, 126, 138, 154
Politburo 106
population ageing 105
population bulge 102
population growth 21, 22, 31, 34, 35, 37, 40, 41, 57, 64, 88, 102-4, 108, 118, 127
positive self-perception 6
powerhouse within the powerhouse 102
pre-teenage girls 153
primary and manufacturing sectors 91, 93
Princess Sayako 46
productivity 2, 8, 108
progressive social policies 87
purchasing power 56, 85

R
rapid urbanization 123
real estate assets 51
reasons for travel 150
recreation and entertainment 56, 68, 76, 79, 84, 99, 115, 122, 125, 130, 134
recreational and leisure activities 138
retired empty nesters 20, 90, 105
retirement 12, 50, 95, 96, 102, 105, 106
rising economic clout of women 73
rural households 108, 118
rural migration 108

S

Sakai, Junko 46
Samsung 9
self-perceptions 102
senior travelers 152
senior women travelers 154
service innovations 80
service sector 52, 61-3, 74, 77, 91-5
service sector employment 95
service sector jobs 94
services 18, 24, 54, 61, 63, 77, 78, 91, 93, 94, 96, 99, 100, 114, 123
Shanghai, Greater Shanghai 106
Shenzhen 106
Shigeaki, Hinohara 51
short-term holiday departures 148
Sichuan 106
Silent Generation 12
silver aristocrats 51, 52
single elderly women 47
single-person households 47
small and medium enterprises (SMEs) 74
small business 62, 132
Smart Woman's Guide to Business Travel 149
social and economic equality 2
Social Transformation 11, 106
spending patterns 48, 68, 99, 119
spending power 53-6, 66, 67, 74, 75, 78, 79, 83, 84, 97-9, 102, 113-5, 119, 120, 121, 123, 124, 128, 129, 130, 132, 133, 138, 139, 142, 145, 155, 156
status 5, 20, 49, 63, 65, 106, 154
staying single 101, 112
structural shift in the economy 96, 123
structural transformation of the economy 77
supermarkets and hypermarkets 138
Switzerland 151

T

tech-savvy women 148
tertiary education, tertiary education levels 3, 4, 88, 102, 132
total consumption power 128
tourism 132, 149
traditional savings deposits 110
transportation and communications 52, 56, 100
travel agencies 132, 150
travel attitudes and trends 148
travel markets of the USA and Europe 147

U

U Curve 52
UK 151
unemployment rate 2, 3
university admission 49
unmarried younger women 47
urban and rural women 118, 123
urban areas 41, 53, 64, 105, 109, 111, 118, 119, 123, 132
urban culture 108
urban households 108, 110, 122
urban hubs 108
urban leisure lifestyles, urban lifestyles 77, 80, 110, 112, 115
urban women consumers 115
urban workers 108
urban young singles 110
urban youth 110
urbanization, education and expansion of manufacturing sector 106
urbanized society 52, 64, 72

V

visitor arrivals 146, 148, 155

W

wholesale and retail 63, 77, 93, 123
winner dogs 46
wired generation 140
women in middle aged households 75, 78, 83, 113, 128, 133, 134
women travelers 146, 148, 149, 150-2, 154, 155
women young singles 81
women's consumption power 50
women's labor force participation rate 50, 123
women's participation 1, 3, 48, 92, 119
women's priorities 92
women's social and economic mobility 108
women-oriented wealth management 99
women-specific travel websites 148
working age empty nesters 91, 105
working empty nesters 46, 74, 75, 78, 79, 81, 83, 84, 98
working empty nesters women households 66
Wuhan 111

Y

young households 18, 23, 25-9, 30, 32, 34-9, 40, 53-5, 66-8, 74-9, 81, 83, 84, 98, 99, 113-5, 119, 120, 121, 123-5, 128, 129, 130, 132-4, 140-2
young married with young child 18
young married, young married households 18, 29, 32, 34, 36, 64, 90, 96, 104, 113, 119, 140
young single women 111, 119
young singles 13, 18, 25, 27, 32, 36, 40, 53, 63, 66, 81, 83, 90, 97, 99, 105, 110-4, 119, 136, 140, 141
young singles households 65
young women, young women households 29, 34, 38, 40, 41, 55, 66, 83, 100, 106, 112, 119, 137, 140, 141
younger women 46, 61, 96, 119
youngest population in Asia 38
Youth League Committee of Beijing Municipality 104

FORTHCOMING TITLES FROM MASTERCARD

0-470-82207-4

0-470-82208-2

0-470-82210-4

The Glittering Silver Market: The Rise of the Elderly Consumers in Asia examines the current elderly consumer markets in Japan, Korea, China, Taiwan, Hong Kong SAR, India, Singapore, Malaysia, Thailand, Indonesia, the Philippines and Australia; and forecasts where they will be in 10 years' time.

The Future and Me: Power of the Youth Market in Asia is a comprehensive assessment of the attitudes and buying patterns of young consumers. This indepth demographic profile identifies the trends and opportunities that are vital to marketers seeking to capitalize on the youth market.

Succeeding Like Success: The Elite Consumers of Asia — Elite, elusive and envied, *Succeeding Like Success* offers a fresh understanding of the elite consumer's motivation and behavior across the region.